The Spice Companion

APPLE

First published in the UK in 2016 by
APPLE PRESS
74-77 White Lion Street
London N1 9PF
United Kingdom

www.apple-press.com

This book was designed, conceived and produced by
Quantum Books Ltd
6 Blundell Street
London N7 9BH
United Kingdom

Publisher: Kerry Enzor
Project Editor: Alison Candlin
Art Editor: Louise Turpin
Illustration: Andrew Pinder
Cover Design: Rupert Gowar-Cliffe and Tokiko Morishima
Production Manager: Zarni Win

ISBN 978-1-84543-648-3

Toppan Leefung Printers Limited, printed in China

2 4 6 8 10 9 7 5 3 1

QUMTHC2

The material in this book has previously appeared
as *The Spice Companion*, by Richard Craze,
published in 2000 by Quintet Publishing Ltd.

The Spice Companion

The Essential Guide to Using Spices in the Kitchen and Home

Edited by Alison Candlin

Contents

List of Spices by Common Name   6

Introduction   8

Directory of Spices   12

Cooking with Spices   110

Spices for Beauty & Health   142

Glossary   156

Index   157

List of Spices by Common Name

ALLSPICE	*Pimento officinalis*	86
ANISEED (ANISE)	*Pimpinella anisum*	88
ASAFETIDA	*Ferula assafoetida*	60
CAPERS	*Capparis spinosa*	28
CAPSICUM (SWEET PEPPERS)	*Capsicum annuum*	30
CARAWAY	*Carum carvi*	40
CARDAMOM	*Elettaria cardamomum*	56
CASSIA	*Cinnamomum cassia*	42
CAYENNE PEPPER	*Capsicum longum*	34
CELERY AND WILD CELERY	*Apium graveolens*	22
CHILLIES	*Capsicum frutescens*	32
CINNAMON	*Cinnamomum zeylanicum*	44
CLOVES	*Eugenia caryophyllus*	58
CORIANDER	*Coriandrum sativum*	46
CUBEB	*Piper cubeba*	90
CUMIN	*Cuminum cyminum*	50
CURRY LEAF	*Murrya koenigii*	72
DILL	*Anethum graveolens*	20
ELECAMPANE	*Inula helenium*	68
FENNEL	*Foeniculum vulgare*	62
FENUGREEK	*Trigonella foenum-graecum*	102
GALANGAL (see Lesser Galangal)		
GINGER	*Zingiber officinale*	108
GRAINS OF PARADISE	*Aframomum melegueta*	14
HORSERADISH	*Armoracia rusticana*	24
JAVA GALANGAL	*Alpinia galanga*	16

Juniper (*above*)	*Juniperus communis*	70
Lemongrass	*Cymbopogon citratus*	54
Lesser Galangal	*Alpinia officinarum*	18
Licorice	*Glycyrrhiza glabra*	64
Mace	*Myristica fragrans*	74
Mustard	*Brassica nigra, B. juncea, B. hirta*	26
Myrtle	*Myrtus communis*	78
Nigella	*Nigella sativa*	80
Nutmeg	*Myristica fragrans*	76
Paprika	*Capsicum tetragonum*	36
Pepper	*Piper nigrum*	92
Poppy	*Papaver somniferum*	82
Quassia	*Picraena excelsa*	84
Safflower	*Carthamus tinctorius*	38
Saffron	*Crocus sativus*	48
Sesame	*Sesamum indicum*	96
Star Anise	*Illicium verum*	66
Sumac	*Rhus coriaria*	94
Sweet Peppers (see Capsicum)		
Szechuan Pepper	*Zanthoxylum piperitum*	106
Tamarind	*Tamarindus indica*	100
Turmeric	*Curcuma longa*	52
Vanilla (*below*)	*Vanilla planifolia*	104
White Mustard	*Sinapis alba*	98

Introduction

Spices are, strictly speaking, the dried parts of aromatic plants – the seeds, flowers, leaves, bark or roots – although a few are used fresh. But there is something evocative about spices that goes way beyond their culinary or medicinal uses. Who can hear the words 'Spice Islands' without feeling a shiver of excitement, a call of adventure and discovery? Some spices are worth more than precious metals and gems; both frankincense and myrrh were considered so valuable that they were included in the three gifts the Wise Men brought to the baby Jesus.

Spices are essential ingredients in any good cook's kitchen. They are also used in the manufacture of incense, oils, cosmetics, preservatives and flavourings. But what exactly is a spice? A precise definition is difficult because some plants are regarded by some people as spices, while other people would argue that they are not. Take garlic, for instance. Is it a spice? It is certainly aromatic and spicy tasting – but it does not grow in the tropics, which is where most spices come from. The word 'spice' usually means the dried seeds of certain hot aromatic plants – but what about sweet peppers? We certainly use their dried fruit in paprika, but we also use the fresh flesh – as we do for chillies. Maybe it is all in the taste. But then we would have to discount turmeric, which has little in the way of a spicy taste but nevertheless is regarded the world over as a spice; certain dishes would be lost without its brilliant yellow colour. In this guide we have included all the traditional spices – as well as a few you may never have heard of but that are still regarded as important in their own countries.

Elecampane root has a strong, bitter taste.

World history without the history of spices would be impossible. Spices have been directly responsible for wars, trade routes, the discovery of America, papal edicts and decrees, medicinal cures, cosmetic preparations and religious rituals, not to mention some of the most tasteful cuisine. And they have been traded and used for longer than most people would think.

Another essential in the rise in use of spices was the invention of the cooking stove. No longer did humans need to cook everything in one pot; they could use several pans – and this meant variety, experimentation and a vast explosion in the use of spices. As the

Spanish explorers returned from the New World, they brought not only gold but also spices never heard of before – and they spread across Europe quickly. There would have been no need for this if spices were used only to flavour meat on its way to going bad – there were already sufficient spices to do that. They spread because people the world over like their food to have a taste, to deliver a surprise, to be interesting and rich.

Now they are the indispensable ingredients in all types of dishes, adding and enhancing existing flavours while at the same time aiding digestion. They complement almost any type of meal, from salads, casseroles and soups to sweet dishes, cakes, pickles and drinks.

Nigella seeds can aid digestion.

But after the ferocious spice trading that went on during the last 600 years, the situation today may seem a little tame. Spices seem to have gradually gone out of favour – no longer do we seek new spice routes or wage war over them. Maybe we have grown used to the less-than-fresh, commercially prepared spices that can be bought in any supermarket. Perhaps it is time to grind a few for ourselves and reawaken our taste buds to the rich aromas and pungent qualities of fresh spices. Or maybe, thanks to the introduction of the fridge into virtually every household in the Western world, we have so much fresh food that we no longer need spices to mask the taste of less palatable or degrading food. Spices, however, are worthy of far more than acting as a cover up – they provide a varied and scintillating range of tastes and experiences.

Spices are no longer regarded as wonders of medicine, but they still play an important part in the manufacture of many cosmetics and perfumes and are grown commercially for their colouring and preservative properties.

The Spice Directory pages of this book comprise a comprehensive illustrated reference, in alphabetical order by botanical name. It covers both common and lesser-known spices, from ginger, cinnamon and pepper, spices that we're all familiar with, to allspice, elecampane and quassia – all shown in the many different forms in which the spices are available – fresh, dried or ground. You will also find pages with ideas for cooking with spices and ways to use spices to boost your health, beauty and help with relaxation.

One or two of the spices may need to be used with some caution – especially the chillies. You can experiment and discard any you do not like, but there will not be many of those. These are the best spices the world has to offer. These are spices to improve the dullest cooking; spices to blend and try; spices to find out about and perhaps use for the first time. Most people have the ubiquitous black pepper mill in the kitchen. Now is the time to go out and buy several more – and grind your own spices in them. We have included the traditional medicinal uses of spices, but you should refer any ailment or condition to a qualified medical doctor before attempting to treat anything yourself at home. We have also included culinary uses, the history of each spice and its origins. There may even be a recipe or two to delight and surprise you.

MEASUREMENTS IN THIS BOOK

All recipe ingredients are given in metric units with imperial measurements in brackets, or in spoon measures.

Abbreviations used are the following:
tsp teaspoon
tbsp tablespoon
ml millilitre
l litre
g gram
oz ounce
fl oz fluid ounce
kg kilogram
m metre
ft foot
F Fahrenheit
C Celsius

A **teaspoon** is 5ml and a **tablespoon** is 15ml. Always use level spoonfuls, not heaped or rounded.

5g (approx.) = 2 tsp (approx.)
10g = 4 tsp = 20ml
40g = 5 tbsp = 80ml

Oven temperatures are not usually given because they can vary so much. However, we would recommend a moderate heat of 180°–190°C (350°–375°F).

*You can make a spicy
lime pickle with chilli,
bay leaves and peppercorns.*

Directory of Spices

Spices have been in use for as long as humans have been cooking and as long as herbal medicine has been around – which may be even longer. They add and enhance flavours in all types of dishes, while at the same time aiding digestion. A few may need to be used with caution – especially the chillies – but experiment with all that the spice world has to offer and find your favourites. These pages list both common and lesser-known spices, showing the different forms in which they are available and explaining their uses in cooking and traditional medicine. Always consult a qualified medical practitioner before treating ailments yourself at home.

Grains of Paradise
Aframomum melegueta

The western African tree *Aframomum melegueta* produces orchid-like, trumpet-shaped flowers in a beautiful yellow or pink with a yellow flash, which in turn produce brilliant scarlet fruits. It is from these that we get the tiny brown seeds of grains of paradise, which are a very unusual, almost pyramid-like shape. They are also known as melegueta pepper and Guinea grains. Related to cardamom, this spice was once used in place of pepper when the price of pepper became too high.

Origins & Characteristics

Originally from western Africa, grains of paradise are widely used in both African and Caribbean cooking. The tree grows only about 2.5m (8ft) tall and is related to both ginger and cardamom. Grains of paradise were certainly known and used in ancient Rome as well as medieval Europe as a pepper substitute. In Britain they were banned by King George III (1760–1820), who believed that peppers or any such hot spices were bad for a person's health.

Culinary Uses

Because the flavour of grains of paradise is hot, spicy and aromatic, they can be used to flavour any dishes in which you would traditionally use black pepper. They can be used in a pepper mill to make an unusual alternative condiment.

If you are able to buy the whole seeds from a West Indian or African grocer, you can then grind them yourself in a pepper mill or pestle and mortar.

Medical Uses

In western Africa the seeds are used internally for a wide range of ailments including painful menstruation and excessive lactation. The root of the tree is cooked and used as a treatment for infertility. The best-known use for the seeds is as an aphrodisiac – but you will have to try them out yourself to see if they work.

Grains of paradise seeds taper to a point, like a pyramid.

🍲 Spicy Jarlsberg Bake

There are several species of grains of paradise. *A. angustifolium* is one of them, and you can cook meat with this pepper.

You will need:
- 800g (2lb) any meat
- handful of grains of paradise
- 250g (9oz) Jarlsberg cheese
- 2 tsp French mustard
- 1 tsp cloves
- 125ml (4fl oz) double cream

Place the meat in thin slices in a baking tray and sprinkle with ground grains of paradise. Mix the cheese, mustard, cloves and cream and spread over the meat. Bake at 200°C (400°F) for 10 minutes (or until meat is cooked through), then grill until golden brown. Serve hot.

The seeds of the grains of paradise tree make a good alternative to black pepper.

Java Galangal
Alpinia galanga

Galangal originated in China, where it is called *Liang-tiang*. However, the Java variety, greater galangal is slightly different from lesser galangal (*Alpinia officinarum*), see page 18. This is a much bigger plant, growing 3m (10ft) tall, with roots more than 1m (3ft) long. Java galangal is cultivated in Indonesia and Malaysia, where it is used to add a ginger-like flavour to curries and savoury meat dishes. In Indonesia it is known as *laos* and in Thailand as *khaa*. In Asian markets it may be sold under any of these names. It is also known as galingale and and Siamese ginger.

Origins & Characteristics

The rhizomes (underground stems of the plant) are harvested in the autumn and washed and dried before use. Knobbly and very like those of ginger in appearance, they have a pungent taste and smell like roses.

The rhizomes are lifted, cleaned and then processed in a similar way to both ginger and turmeric. The powdered root is then often mixed with other powdered spices.

Culinary Uses

You can add the powdered root to curries and stews. Because it is subtler than lesser galangal (page 18), it has a more delicate flavour and is suitable for people who prefer a milder curry. It can be used to flavour sausages. The oil can be extracted and used to flavour soft drinks, liqueurs and bitters. The powdered root can be used in any dish in which you might traditionally use fresh ginger.

Medicinal Uses

Java galangal is a warming digestive and is used as a remedy for diarrhoea, gastric upsets and incontinence. In Asia it is used to treat respiratory problems and congestion, and a drink of grated galangal mixed with lime juice is regarded as a tonic in Southeast Asia. The English variety of galangal, *Cyperus longus*, is used, according to the English physician Nicholas Culpeper (1616–1654), for expelling wind, strengthening the bowels, helping colic, provoking urine and preventing dropsy. It is also said to be good for fainting spells.

Galangal root looks a lot like ginger and is used in a similar way.

🍵 JAVA GALANGAL TEA

You will need:
• 25g (1oz) powdered root
• 500ml (18fl oz) boiling water

To make Java galangal tea, place the powdered root in a pot and add the water. Steep for half an hour, then strain and let cool. Sip 2 tbsp at a time. This is thought to be a good remedy for liver complaints such as hepatitis and cirrhosis and stomach and digestion upsets.

The rhizomes are the useful part of the stately Java galangal plant.

Lesser Galangal
Alpinia officinarum

This is the strong Chinese variety of galangal. Its taste and effects are less subtle, and it is a smaller plant than Java galangal (page 16), growing only to around 1.5m (5ft) tall. It has been an essential ingredient in Chinese herbal medicine since at least A.D. 500 and is also known as just 'galangal' and China root. In China it is called *sa leung geung*, while its Southeast Asian name is *kencur*.

Origins & Characteristics
The lesser galangal has spikes of wonderful orchid-like white flowers with red streaks. The roots are washed and dried before they are powdered; they are brown on the outside and orange on the inside. Galangal has been known to the West since the time of the Crusades in the thirteenth century, when the knights brought the root back from their travels. In Tudor and medieval times, it was used extensively in cooking and as an ingredient in perfume, but it fell out of favour by the eighteenth century.

Today it is valued in the West only as a medicine, although in China it is still an important ingredient in soups and stews – it is valued for its warming, ginger-like effect.

Culinary Uses
You can add the powdered root of galangal to any savoury dish in which you would use fresh ginger – the taste and effect are very similar. It makes a useful substitute if you cannot get fresh ginger.

Medicinal Uses
Galangal is taken internally for chronic gastritis, digestive upsets and gastric ulcerations, and to relieve the pain of rheumatism. The powdered root can be used to make a poultice that may help to relieve the itch and irritation of skin infections.

A tea thought to relieve the pain of gum disorders and mouth ulcers can be made by adding 25g (1oz) to 500ml (18fl oz) of hot water and letting it stand for an hour. A tablespoon at a time can be used as a gargle and mouthwash. This tea can be drunk, a tablespoon at a time, to relieve flatulence and indigestion.

Powdered galangal root is often mixed with other spices.

🍲 SPINACH AND GALANGAL BHAJI

You will need:
- 800g (1¾lb) cooked spinach
- 1 medium onion
- 60g (2oz) butter
- 4 dried red chillies
- 1 tsp cumin seeds
- 2 tsp ground galangal powder
- salt

Chop then fry the onion in the butter and add to the spinach. Then add the chillies, cumin seeds and galangal powder and cook over low heat for 10 minutes. Add salt to taste.

Lesser galangal grows to only half the size of Java galangal.

Dill
Anethum graveolens

The common name for dill comes from the old Norse word *dilla*, which means 'to lull' – and dill's mild sedative effect certainly lulls digestive discomfort in children and adults alike. Dill water, commonly known as gripe water, has been used for centuries to soothe colicky and fretful small babies. It was once, in medieval times, thought to be a magic herb and, as such, was used to combat witchcraft. It was also used in love potions for the same reason. Both the seeds and the leaves are used. Nowadays it is mostly grown in the Northern Hemisphere.

Origins & Characteristics

Dill is a native of northern Europe and Russia but is now cultivated throughout the world. It is a tall, spindly plant that grows nearly 2m (6½ft) tall, with slender stems and fine leaves. The tiny yellow flowers turn into winged seeds at the end of the summer. Both the flowers and seeds are harvested.

Culinary Uses

Dill seeds are strong tasting and warming. They taste similar to caraway, and they can be used to flavour cakes and desserts. You can also use them as a pickling spice for vinegars.

The leaves have a less strong flavour and are slightly less bitter. You can add the finely chopped fresh leaves to any fish dishes, salads and soured cream sauces.

If you use the leaves in any hot dishes, add them near the end of the cooking time to preserve the flavour.

Dill seeds are tiny, but have a powerful flavour.

Medicinal Uses

Dill is rich in sulfur, potassium and sodium and is considered by herbalists to be a completely safe plant. To make gripe water, steep a teaspoon of partly crushed seeds in a glass of hot water for two hours. Strain and add honey for flavour. Make sure it is completely cool before giving it to a baby and give only a teaspoon at a time.

Adults are also said to benefit from gripe water if they have upset stomachs because dill is a good aid to digestion; it may also stimulate appetite and help promote milk production in nursing mothers. The seeds can be chewed raw to sweeten the breath and can also act as a digestive aid.

Harvesting & Storage

Pick the fresh leaves at any time to add to your cooking, but to harvest the seeds, pick the flower heads when they are part flower and part seed. Hang the heads upside down in a dry place over a cloth to catch the seeds as they fall. Sow the seeds in a sunny but sheltered garden. Do not plant them near fennel because the two can cross-pollinate.

Leaves and flowerheads are used in cooking and medicine.

Celery and Wild Celery
Apium graveolens

From wild celery, also known as smallage, that grows throughout Europe in river estuaries and salt marshes, we get cultivated celery, whose crisp stems and leaves can be used in salads and cooked with meat stews and casseroles. Smallage, once used as a medicine, would taste very bitter to the modern palate, but the Romans found it useful as a flavouring and it is these seeds that are used as a spice. They are warming and aromatic but quite bitter to taste.

Origins & Characteristics
Wild celery seeds have been found in the tomb of Tutankhamun, suggesting that their medicinal benefits have been known for thousands of years. Culpeper – a seventeenth century English herbalist, botanist and physician – says that the seed 'helps the dropsy and jaundice and removes female obstructions' and that the leaves are of the same nature and 'eaten in the spring sweeten and purify the blood and help the scurvy'.

Culinary Uses
The seeds of wild celery are quite strong and bitter, so you need only very small quantities. They can be used whole to flavour soups and stews or ground and mixed with salt and used as a condiment.
   To make a warming and spicy tea, grind ½ tsp of seeds and add to 250ml (9fl oz) of hot water. Steep for 10 minutes and drink it while it's still warm. The juice of cultivated celery stalk can be extracted in a food processor and drunk cool. Celery salt, a salt-based seasoning flavoured with the essential oil, is more widely available but soon develops a stale taste.

Medicinal Uses
A poultice for external use can be made from celery leaves to relieve fungal infections, and the seeds taken internally in small quantities are said to be good for relieving gout, arthritis and inflammation of the urinary tract. Eating the seeds of raw cultivated celery, either by chewing or swallowing them whole, is said to lower blood pressure, to stimulate digestion and to treat rheumatism.

When ground, celery seeds make a warm and spicy tea.

Growing

To grow your own wild or cultivated celery, plant the seeds in rich, damp soil in a sunny but sheltered position in the spring. The plants do not like frost and will not flower until their second year. Once they have flowered, they will produce seeds readily. The stems of the cultivated celery are best picked and used in the autumn, traditionally after the first frost.

Caution

The seeds of cultivated celery sold for cultivation should not be used for medicinal purposes because they may well have been treated with fungicides.

A poultice of celery leaves can be used to treat fungal infections.

Horseradish
Armoracia rusticana

Horseradish originated in eastern Europe and is a good kitchen garden plant because its root can be used in a variety of ways to season food. It does need to be contained, however, as it spreads rapidly and, once established, can be a nightmare to eradicate. The root has an extremely powerful flavour. It is used to make the well-known horseradish sauce, in which the combination of ingredients brings out the root's qualities to the best advantage. A homemade sauce is much more flavourful than the commercial variety.

Discard the leaves and flowers; the root is the powerhouse of the horseradish plant.

Origins & Characteristics

Horseradish is a perennial, dark green plant with white flowers. The young leaves can be used for flavouring, but it is the root that most people associate with horseradish. The root has to be dug up fresh because it does not store or keep well.

Culinary Uses

The fresh root has a strong, eye-watering pungency (overpowering for some people) and a powerful and stimulating flavour. The fresh root should be grated – carefully to prevent any juice from getting into the eyes – and then added to cream and vinegar to make a sauce that can be used to add zest to fish and, traditionally, roast beef. It makes a good accompaniment to hard-boiled eggs and is delicious with smoked mackerel.

You can make the root a little milder by adding apple to it when you are grating it. You can also warm the sauce, but do so very gently because too much heat destroys the oils that give it its pungency.

Medicinal Uses

Horseradish is a diuretic, which increases urinary flow. It increases perspiration as well, which can be good for some fevers, and it can be made into a poultice to be used externally for wound infections, arthritis and pleurisy.

The considerable warming effect of horseradish can cause skin irritation in certain circumstances, and if too much is taken internally, it can cause vomiting and may provoke allergic reactions. Taken internally, it can relieve gout and arthritis as well as urinary and respiratory infections. It should not be given to anyone with stomach ulcers or thyroid problems.

Grated horseradish root has a fiery flavour.

Mustard
Brassica nigra, B. juncea, B. hirta

There are so many varieties of mustard and so much can be made from this one plant that cooks may not need any other kitchen spices. *Brassica nigra* is the black mustard, now only grown in peasant economies, which has been replaced in large-scale farming by *B. juncea*, brown or Indian mustard. White mustard, *B. hirta*, is also sometimes known as *Sinapsis alba*. In medieval times mustard was the only spice that the general populace could afford and being in such common use, mustard has given us some interesting language – 'as keen as mustard', 'cutting the mustard' and, from the Bible, 'The kingdom of heaven is like to a grain of mustard seed'.

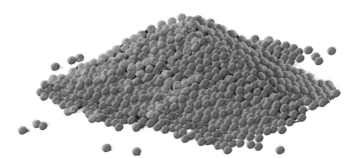

Brown mustard seeds (above) and black mustard seeds (right).

Origins & Characteristics

Mustard has been grown for so long that its origins are lost, but it probably came from the eastern Mediterranean, where it grows as a weed and is used for feeding horses.

It is a spindly plant that grows around 1m (3ft) tall, with bright yellow flowers. The seeds are usually brown or reddish. Real mustard was originally made with fresh grape juice, or the 'must', from the Latin word *mustum*, hence its name.

Culinary Uses

The young leaves can be cooked as a vegetable, and the flowers can be added to summer salads. The seeds are ground and used as a fiery spice for making mustard, which accompanies many dishes from cold meats to cheeses and is used in sauces for hot dishes. It is also used in vinaigrette dressing. You can use it to add a certain piquancy to sauces for macaroni or baked cauliflower with cheese.

Dry mustard powder releases its pungency when it comes into contact with cold liquid. If you use hot liquids when making up mustard, the pungency is reduced or even eliminated altogether – so always make your mustard with cold water or vinegar.

The whole seeds can be used to flavour especially hot curries and for pickling. (See pages 138–9 for additional information.)

Medicinal Uses

Traditionally, mustard plasters were applied as poultices to relieve rheumatism, muscular pain and chilblains. You can soak your feet by wrapping the plaster, soaked in mustard, around them to ease aches and strains. Mustard plasters may also provide relief for headaches and colds. Remember to use cold water to maximise the heating effect.

Caution

People with sensitive skin should take care when using mustard plasters because they can cause blistering. In large doses mustard causes vomiting.

Capers
Capparis spinosa

In southern Europe the pickled caper has been used as a condiment for at least the last 2,000 years. The characteristic flavour comes from the capric acid that develops when the flower buds are pickled in vinegar. Capers are used widely in North African cooking as well as in cooking throughout the whole of the Mediterranean – they are especially loved in Sardinia. Increasingly used in the West, they can make a surprising and useful addition to salads or be used as pizza toppings.

Origins & Characteristics

Capers grow wild throughout the Mediterranean, where they are regarded as weeds. The plant has thick, shiny leaves and short-lived flowers that have purple stamens and fringed white petals streaked with pale pink. It is a beautiful plant and can be grown in temperate climates if it is grown under glass in well-drained soil.

Culinary Uses

The whole pickled caper buds are used in casseroles, stews and lamb dishes as well as in ravigote, tartar and remoulade sauces. They are a good complement to any oily fish and are especially good eaten with salty foods such as salted meat or fish. Capers add an unexpected but refreshing taste to food. They can be added to parsley and sprinkled over beef. They are an essential ingredient in tapenade, which is an olive paste made in the Mediterranean, and in caponata, which is a Sardinian salad of aubergine and tuna.

Medicinal Uses

Capers can increase digestion and appetite and induce a general feeling of well-being and vitality. They are thought to be good for gastrointestinal infections and diarrhoea. The flower buds can be infused in a tea to help to ease coughs.

Storage

Capers should be kept in a tightly lidded glass jar. Always make sure that they are kept immersed in the vinegar in which they were pickled; otherwise, they will dry out and lose their flavour. It is also best to keep them stored in a dark place.

Capers look like berries, but are the flower buds of the plant.

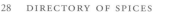

🍲 CAPER SAUCE

You will need:
- 15g (½oz) butter
- 1 tbsp flour
- 250ml (9fl oz) milk
- 1 tbsp chopped capers
- 1 tsp vinegar in which capers were pickled

Melt the butter in a small saucepan and gradually beat in the flour with a wooden spoon. Add the milk little by little, stirring all the time until the sauce is of a medium thick consistency. Then add capers and their vinegar.

Caper buds are picked and pickled before the flowers open.

Capsicum (Sweet Peppers)
Capsicum annuum

Like chillies (page 32), these too are named from the Latin word *capsa*, meaning 'box', and a pepper is a 'box' of seeds. They are milder and more flavourful than chillies and can be eaten raw without any ill effects or burning sensations. They are fresh and juicy with a clear tangy texture. Red ones are also known as pimentos.

Origins & Characteristics
Sweet peppers are originally from tropical America but are now cultivated the world over in warm climates. They grow on bushes about 1m (3ft) tall, with white flowers. The fruits start off green and slowly turn red or yellow as they mature, but the green, immature ones can be used in the same manner as the red or yellow ones.

Culinary Uses
Sweet peppers can be sliced and added raw to salads or used as a salad vegetable on their own. They can be sliced and fried to add to meat sauces. The seeds should be removed before using.

The dried and ground flesh of sweet peppers is made into paprika (page 36). Before cooking sweet peppers, check them for freshness because they go bad easily. Feel for any soft spots and notice any patches of black or brown discolouration.

Peppers are excellent pickled or in chutneys and are one of the main ingredients, along with courgette and aubergine, in French ratatouille (aubergine, courgette, peppers, tomatoes,

etc. cooked in olive oil). The red peppers are sweetest, and the green ones can be quite bitter. You can blanch them for two or three minutes before using to improve the flavour. Peppers can be grilled until they blister and then eaten as a side dish.

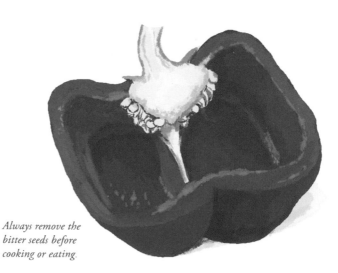

Always remove the bitter seeds before cooking or eating.

Medicinal Uses

Sweet peppers contain large amounts of vitamin C, so they are very good for you. They also have revitalising and antiseptic qualities and are used to stimulate the digestive system.

🥘 ANDALUSIAN GAZPACHO

You will need:
- 4 green peppers
- 4 large tomatoes
- ½ seedless cucumber
- 150g (5oz) white bread crumbs
- 250ml (9fl oz) olive oil
- 1l (1¾ pints) water
- salt and black pepper
- 2 garlic cloves, crushed
- 1 tsp white wine vinegar

Finely chop the peppers, tomatoes and cucumber. Add to the breadcrumbs with a large helping of olive oil. Add the water to this mixture and leave for one hour. Put through a food processor or blender. Add salt and pepper to taste. Add the garlic to the vinegar, and pour over the mixture and refrigerate until well chilled. Serve cold.

Chillies
Capsicum frutescens

Although chillies are related to sweet pepper (page 30), there is a considerable difference – mainly the heat. Chillies range in colour from red to purple, cream, yellow, green and even black. There is an old saying that the smaller they are, the hotter they are, but be careful – some of the larger ones are really very hot indeed.

Chilli pepper fruits come in a range of different colours.

Origins & Characteristics

Chillies were brought to Europe by Spanish explorers returning from South America and are now cultivated throughout the world. There is evidence that they have been grown and used in Central and South America for at least 9,000 years. They can be grown in temperate climates, but they need artificial heat. They grow 2m (6½ft) tall, with tiny slender fruits that, when dried, are used as the main ingredient in cayenne pepper and Tabasco sauce. The fresh fruit itself is used in Mexican cooking; generally the seeds are taken out before use. Chillies are best used fresh.

Culinary Uses

Fresh chillies are used in guacamole, mole poblano and Yucatan soup. They can be grilled until the flesh begins to smoke and blister and then eaten hot – but caution should be used because the chillies can be an irritant. Chillies should be washed under cold water to reduce their fieriness. Indian chillies are used in curries to give them that extra hot quality. Chilli powder is cayenne powder (a blend of small, ripe chillies of various origins) mixed with cumin and marjoram or garlic.

Medicinal Uses

Chillies are used to revive the body, and they are said to help the digestion and to have a strong stimulant effect. They are warming for colds and chills, and they have excellent antibacterial properties.

Caution

Chillies are a very powerful eye and skin irritant – use thin rubber gloves whenever you are handling them fresh. If any of the juice gets on your skin, wash it off immediately with large amounts of cold milk or soap and water. If it should get in your eyes, flush them with generous amounts of cool water. Taken in excess, chillies cause damage to the mucous membranes, as well as digestive and renal problems.

Dried and crushed, including the seeds, chilli makes a powerful flavouring.

Cayenne Pepper
Capsicum longum

If you dry fresh chillies and grind them up, you have the makings of cayenne pepper – from which you can make hot sauce and chilli powder. Also known as *lal mirch* in India and *pisihui* in Southeast Asia, cayenne is also added to ointments for the treatment of neuralgia, chilblains and lumbago. This is because the chillies contain capsaicin, which is a chemical found to increase blood circulation on contact. As their name suggests, *Capsicum longum* are long and thin – and very hot.

Origins & Characteristics
The usual story told about cayenne pepper is that it was used by the cooks of chuck wagons on the cattle drives across the Texas plains to flavour some pretty unsavoury meats – such as rattlesnake. A lot of the cooks sowed seeds of various plants along the cattle trails so that they could have fresh herbs and spices in later years. This is why there has been such a spread of spices growing wild in the United States. Some of these may well have originally not been native plants.

Culinary Uses
Cayenne pepper is used in hot dishes such as chilli con carne. Cayenne can be added to any savoury meat dishes in which you want to add heat without necessarily adding extra flavour. You can also add the merest pinch to cheese sauces and spicy mayonnaise (instead of mustard) to give them added colour.

Medicinal Uses
You can infuse cayenne to make a hot, fiery tea thought to stimulate the appetite, relieve stomach and bowel pains and ease cramps. A poultice of cayenne is said to relieve rheumatism and lumbago.

Caution
A poultice of cayenne may cause a reaction in people with sensitive skin.

Cayenne pepper is as hot and fiery as its colour suggests.

Cayenne is made by drying and grinding fresh chillies (above).

🍲 CHILLI CON CARNE

You will need:
- 400g (14oz) kidney beans
- 1 small onion
- 10g (⅓oz) butter
- 1 garlic clove, crushed
- 750g (1¾lb) minced beef
- 200g (8oz) chopped tomatoes
- 2tsp cayenne pepper

Whether chilli con carne should have beans in it and whether it can include cayenne pepper or only fresh chillies is debatable, but you can decide which you prefer. Soak the kidney beans overnight and then rinse and boil for 10 minutes; rinse again and boil in salted water until tender, drain and let cool. Chop the onion and fry in the butter and garlic. Add the minced beef and fry together until the beef is browned. Add the tomatoes, kidney beans, cayenne pepper and salt and black pepper to taste. Let simmer for two hours until very thick.

Paprika
Capsicum tetragonum

Paprika is made from sweet peppers that have been dried and ground. Ideally only the dried fruit should be used. It has more flavour – lightly pungent and rather sweet – and a lot less heat than cayenne pepper. Instantly recognisable by its bright red colour, paprika is the traditional ingredient in Hungarian goulash and in many other dishes from that country. It makes a colourful addition to a wide variety of food including meat, vegetables and barbeque spice mixtures. It is also used as an ingredient in Cajun seasoning.

Ground paprika has a distictive, bright red colour.

Origins & Characteristics

Although most people consider Hungary as the natural place for paprika to have originated, it was actually introduced there by the Turks. 'Paprika' is, however, a Hungarian word, and paprika is the national spice of Hungary, where it is treated with almost religious fervour. It is made only from red sweet peppers, and most paprika outside of Hungary has little in the way of hotness. Its bitterness depends on how much seed is used – ideally only the dried fruit should be used to make good paprika – and the lighter in colour the red peppers are, the hotter the spice will be.

Culinary Uses

Paprika is used throughout Europe, especially in Portugal and Spain, but the Hungarians use paprika the most – to flavour and colour many dishes including soups, vegetables, chicken, fish and meat. But it is mostly known throughout the world as the key ingredient in Hungarian goulash, a beef stew. Paprika doesn't keep very well, so it should be bought in small quantities. You can also use it to garnish canapés and in sauces for shellfish and shrimp. It also makes an excellent sauce to serve with lobster or crab.

Medicinal Uses

It was in 1926 that a Hungarian chemist called Szent Gyorgi first isolated vitamin C – from paprika. It is ironic to think of the sailors on the spice routes getting scurvy, which is caused by a lack of vitamin C, when they had access to fresh peppers all the time.

Paprika has warming qualities that are thought to make it effective against cold symptoms, and, together with its supply of vitamin C, it appears to be the perfect antidote to winter.

Sweet peppers or the longer Romano peppers (above) are dried to intensify flavour before being ground into paprika.

Safflower
Carthamus tinctorius

Because it is often called bastard saffron, you might think that safflower is the poor relation of saffron (page 48), but in reality it is an important spice in its own right. However; the more unscrupulous traders will try to sell it as saffron. It has a slightly duller colour than saffron and is more orange – in fact this is the spice that produces the bright orange dye used for Buddhists' robes – they really ought to be called safflower robes. The flowers produce a yellow dye if they are processed in water and a red dye if alcohol is used. Safflower will add colour to food but won't flavour it.

Origins & Characteristics
Safflower has been cultivated for so long that it is impossible to say exactly where it originated. It has been found in Egyptian tombs dating back to at least 3500 B.C. and has been used in traditional Chinese herbal medicine for a very long time. The flowers are a bright orange-yellow and are used for making tea and as a saffron substitute. The oil processed from the seeds is used as a cooking oil, and the seeds themselves can be ground and used as a spice.

Culinary Uses
The oil made from safflower is low in cholesterol, so it is very good for anyone on a low-cholesterol diet. You can use the flowers in any recipe in which you would use saffron – they have a slightly more bitter taste but are considerably less expensive.

Medicinal Uses
The flower petals can be infused to make a tea that is said to be good as a laxative and to induce perspiration and reduce fevers. Safflower taken as a tea is also good for coronary artery disease and menopausal and menstruation problems, although it should not be given to pregnant women. It may help to reduce the symptoms of jaundice and measles.

A poultice made from the flowers is used for reducing skin inflammation and for easing bruises and sprains. Applied externally, the flowers are also said to relieve painful and swollen joints.

Dried safflower petals are best used fresh.

Storage
The flowers only keep for about a year, so they should be used when they are fairly fresh for the best benefit. They will add a gorgeous colour to pot pourri, earning their keep despite their lack of aroma.

Caution
Avoid taking safflower if you are pregnant.

🍵 SAFFLOWER TEA

You will need:
- 1 tsp safflower flowers
- 250ml (9fl oz) hot water

For an infusion, steep the flowers in the water. Taken hot, it may induce perspiration. Taken cool, it is said to soothe hysteria.

Safflower can be used to make yellow or red dye, as well as the orange of Buddhists' robes.

Caraway
Carum carvi

You may not think that such a small, nondescript plant could have so many uses or could be so highly prized as a charm against witchcraft and demons. It was also once believed that anything containing caraway could not be stolen, so it was fed to pigeons to stop them from straying and it was thought that if a wife placed a few of the seeds in her husband's pockets, he could not have his heart stolen away. Caraway was also believed to cure venomous serpent bites, prevent hair loss and restore failing eyesight.

Origins & Characteristics
Caraway grows wild throughout Europe and Asia and has now been naturalised in the United States and Canada. It is cultivated in the Netherlands and Russia on a large scale. It grows only about 20cm (8in) tall, with white or pink flowers.

Culinary Uses
The leaves can be eaten fresh in salads or added chopped to freshly cooked vegetables. You can add the chopped leaves to cream sauces for a warming, mild flavour not unlike parsley. The leaves and stems can be cooked in stews and soups. If the flowers are picked off early enough, the tap roots will grow larger and can be cooked as a vegetable – they taste like parsnips.

The seeds are used to flavour caraway candy, and the oil of the plant is used to make liqueurs such as kummel. The ground seeds are used in curry powder as well as in flavouring for cakes, breads and biscuits. Caraway is very popular in German and Scandinavian cooking. The seeds are even dipped in sugar and eaten as a confection known as sugar plums.

Medicinal Uses
The seeds are chewed for immediate relief of indigestion and colic as well as menstrual pains and cramps. The leaves are used to make a tea that may reduce intestinal and uterine spasms as well as relieve flatulence and indigestion.

Caraway seeds are delicious when gently fried and eaten with apples or cheese.

🥘 Satay Sauce

You will need:
- 1 medium onion, chopped
- 200g (7oz) roasted peanuts
- 3 garlic cloves, crushed
- 1 tsp caraway seeds
- 4 tsp coriander seeds
- 3 tsp turmeric
- ½ tsp cayenne pepper
- 250g (9oz) shredded coconut
- 2 tbsp soy sauce
- 1 tsp honey
- 500ml (18fl oz) water

Blend everything together and simmer, stirring occasionally, until it thickens. Let the sauce stand for half an hour before using as a dip or to marinate meat.

The caraway plant can offer relief from many causes of intestinal discomfort.

Cassia bark tastes a little more robust than cinnamon, but the two are used in the same ways.

Cassia
Cinnamomum cassia

The bark of cassia, also known as Chinese cinnamon, is a form of cinnamon. Indeed, in the United States, it is used and sold simply as 'cinnamon', and in many countries, cassia and cinnamon are used interchangeably. They are closely related, but their taste does differ, cassia being less delicate. It is one of the oldest spices used as a medicine. It was first used in China in 2700 B.C. and in Egypt in 1600 B.C. In Chinese herbal medicine it is known as *gui zhi*. It is native to Assam and northern Burma.

Origins & Characteristics

Cassia grows in most Asian countries, and the bark is dried in quills for powdering and for using in infusions and tinctures. The twigs and leaves are distilled for their oil – cassia oil contains around 85 per cent cinnamaldehyde, which is an important product in the pharmaceutical and food industry. It is also used in the manufacture of cosmetics. The buds are harvested and dried for use as a flavouring in the food industry – they look like cloves.

Culinary Uses

In the United States cassia is used as a sweet spice for flavouring cakes and pastries, while in Asia it is used as a flavouring for curries and savoury meat dishes. It is one of the five ingredients in Chinese five-spice (the others being anise, star anise, cloves and fennel seeds). This mixture is used to flavour roasted meats, poultry and marinades. The predominant flavour, however, is star anise.

Medicinal Uses

In Chinese herbal medicine *gui zhi* is used to treat diarrhoea, poor appetite, coldness, rheumatism, angina, palpitations and digestive complaints. In the West, cassia is a major ingredient in cold remedies, and it is also commonly used to treat dyspepsia, flatulence and colic.

Other Uses

Cassia is sometimes regarded as a poor substitute for cinnamon (page 44). However, it has a stronger taste than cinnamon, and some people find that it tastes sweeter and prefer it to flavour mulled wine and sweets.

The flowers and dried bark can be used in pot pourri. In America cassia is called cinnamon, and in France both barks are known by only one name – *cannelle*. Cassia is much thicker and rougher than true cinnamon and often comes in unrolled lumps, whereas cinnamon usually comes in neat sticks.

Cinnamon
Cinnamomum zeylanicum

Since ancient times the fragrant, dried inner bark of the cinnamon tree has been a valued spice. The Phoenician traders probably brought it to the Middle East, where it has been used as a perfume since Old Testament times – Moses used it as an ingredient in the anointing oil in the tabernacle. Since the ninth century it has been widely used in Europe, and most of the cinnamon that is used today comes from Sri Lanka.

Origins & Characteristics

In its native habitat this bushy evergreen tree can grow very tall indeed. The deeply veined fragrant leaves are long and dark green with lighter undersides. The flowers are yellow and small and turn into dark purple berries. The bark is the part that is used.

Cinnamon can be cultivated from seed or by taking cuttings from a plant. The shoots are cut back every two to three years, and the bark is peeled off and left to dry for a day. The outer bark is then stripped away, and the inner bark rolls itself into tight sticks as it dries.

Culinary Uses

For spicing hot drinks such as punch and mulled wine, whole cinnamon sticks are used. They can be used with stewed or fresh fruit and in fruit punches. You can use the sticks to stir the flavour of cinnamon into other hot drinks.

Medicinal Uses

Cinnamon is a strong stimulant for the glandular system and is used to relieve stomach upset. It is very warming, so it is good for relieving the symptoms of colds, flu and sore throats.

Ground cinnamon does not keep well; store it in an airtight jar.

Storage

Cinnamon is best when bought in sticks, but it can also be bought ground. Ground cinnamon actually tastes stronger, but it should be kept stored in screw-topped glass jars because it loses its smell fairly quickly. The highest quality cinnamon is made from the thinnest bark, which has the best taste and fragrance.

As it dries in the sun, cinnamon bark rolls itself into its distinctive coiled sticks.

Coriander
Coriandrum sativum

Coriander is a small annual herb that grows wild throughout the Mediterranean. It was introduced to China around A.D. 600 and called *hu*, meaning 'foreign'. It is now cultivated in most parts of the world as an important ingredient in the food industry, because it is high in linalol (70 per cent), which is used as a flavouring for vegetables, pickles, seasonings and curries. The name coriander comes from the Greek word *koros*, meaning 'bug' or 'insect', because the fruit has an unpleasant foetid smell before it has ripened. In the United States, the plant is known as cilantro, but the seeds, which are the part of the plant used as a spice, are called coriander.

Origins & Characteristics
Coriander grows well in any well-drained soil as long as it is sunny. It grows about 70cm (2ft) tall with delicate pink and white flowers. It will bolt – grow tall and leggy and run to seed – if left to dry at the seedling stage. Coriander grown in warmer climates has much larger fruit than that grown in more moderate regions.

Culinary Uses
In the Middle East and Asia, especially China, the leaves are used to flavour savoury dishes and the seeds as a pickling spice. The whole seeds can be used in cooking fish as well as in breads and cakes; ground seeds can be added to sausages, curries and roasted meat. In India the seeds are usually lightly toasted before they are ground. The seeds are slightly sweet and have a citrus-like taste.

Medicinal Uses
Coriander leaves are used as a remedy for minor digestive problems, and the seeds can reduce the painful stomach spasm effect of some laxatives. Coriander ointment is used externally to relieve the symptoms of haemorrhoids and painful joints. It also stimulates the appetite and is a mild stomach relaxant.

Cosmetic Uses
A good aftershave can be made by infusing coriander seed in alcohol and adding some honey and orange flower water. If the seeds are harvested in late summer and dried before they are used, the perfume is drawn out. The longer the seeds are kept, the better the scent.

Coriander seeds are used as a spice in a variety of savoury dishes.

*The leaves of the coriander
plant can help to relieve
stomach pains.*

Saffron
Crocus sativus

At times in its history, saffron has been more expensive than gold, and it has the same colour as well – a deep, dark, golden orange. The slender stigmas of the plant are very light and are handpicked, which accounts for saffron's high value. Luckily very little of the spice is needed to impart its wonderful, slightly bitter taste to cooking.

Origins & Characteristics

Saffron is made from the dried stigmas of a blue-flowered crocus, which are handpicked in their native Turkey. The plants also grow in surrounding countries, and the very best saffron is said to come from Valencia. A lot of stigmas (around 200–500) are needed to make a tiny amount (1g) of saffron; that is why it is so expensive.

Purchased saffron comes in two varieties – threads and ground. Ideally you should purchase threads because any artificial dying or colouring is easier to spot in threads.

Safflower stigmas (page 38) are often passed off as saffron, but they are redder in colour and don't have the same taste. Turmeric (page 53) is also sold as saffron, but it is easy to spot because it has quite a different colour and taste.

Culinary Uses

Saffron has been used to both flavour and colour food since ancient times. It is an essential ingredient in paella, bouillabaisse and risotto Milanese, and of course, saffron cakes. You can use saffron in a variety of other dishes; it flavours shellfish and fish well, and it is a useful ingredient in sauces and rice.

Saffron threads should be broken up and infused in a little hot water; the strained liquid should then be added to the dish according to the recipe instructions. Alternatively, you can dry the threads in the oven first and then crumble them into the recipe. The threads should be dark orange with no white streaks. Ground saffron should also be infused before it is used. A mere pinch is enough to flavour rice for four people.

Saffron, the dried stigmas of the crocus flower, is the most expensive spice in the world.

Medicinal Uses

You can infuse saffron to make an herbal tea that is taken as a warming, soothing drink to clear the head. It is also believed to shake off drowsiness and bring on menstruation.

Other Uses

Saffron is also highly effective as a dye for fabric. Just a small amount will turn cloth a beautiful light gold colour.

Caution

Make sure only the stigmas from *Crocus sativus* are used. *Colchicum autumnale* looks very similar but it is poisonous.

Only Crocus sativus *flowers should be used for harvesting saffron.*

Cumin
Cuminum cyminum

Cumin is a native of the Middle East. It is grown for its seed-like fruit, which is a pungent and aromatic spice, similar to caraway (page 40). It is mentioned often in the Bible and is a staunch favourite in Greek, Turkish and Arab cooking. The ancient Romans used cumin as a condiment much like we would use black pepper today, but it is probably best known for its role in Indian cuisine – especially curries and chicken roasted in a tandoor.

Origins & Characteristics
Cumin will grow in any warm, sunny position in rich, well-drained sandy loam. It grows about 60cm (2ft) tall, with very slender stems and tiny pink or white flowers. Indian cumin comes in two varieties – white (*safed*) and black (*kala*). The black cumin has a more subtle flavour but is somewhat expensive and hard to come by outside of India. The fruits are picked before they are fully ripe and left to dry – these are then used ground or whole.

Culinary Uses
Cumin is used in the spice blend garam masala and is an important ingredient of couscous (cracked wheat steamed and served with meat, vegetables, chickpeas and raisins), which is made throughout the Middle East and North Africa. Cumin is used to flavour meats and cheeses – such as Dutch Edam and the German Muenster. In the Middle East the seeds are often roasted and added to lamb dishes as well as to side dishes of cucumber and yogurt.

Medicinal Uses
Cumin is taken internally for minor digestive disorders; it is believed to settle stomach upsets that cause migraines. It is a warming appetite stimulant.

Storage
Ground cumin doesn't store well, so it should be bought in small quantities. Whole seeds are difficult to grind with a mortar, so buy both whole seeds and the ground powder.

Cumin can be bought as seeds (above) or ground into a powder. It isn't easy to grind your own.

Spicy Drink with Cumin

A digestive drink is made in India by mixing mint, ginger, salt, sugar, tamarind water and lemon juice with ground cumin.

You will need:
- sprig of mint
- pinch of ginger
- pinch of salt
- 250ml (9fl oz) tamarind water
- lemon juice
- sugar
- 1 tsp ground cumin

Mix the ginger, cumin and salt into the tamarind water.
Add the lemon juice and sugar to taste. Garnish with the mint.

Cumin is a delicate, slender plant, but its fruits have a strong and pungent flavour.

*Inside, the turmeric root is a
bright orange.*

Turmeric
Curcuma longa

Origins & Characteristics

Turmeric grows about 50cm (2ft) tall, with large broad leaves and yellow flowers. It is a native of India, but it is now cultivated throughout the world, especially China, Java, Peru – and India, of course, where some 12,000 tons of it are produced annually. Most of this is exported.

Culinary Uses

Turmeric is one of the principal ingredients of curry powder. Although its very strong colour is its main attraction, it does have a distinctive taste – like a mild curry flavour, slightly bitter but fragrant. Turmeric is often added to cooking rice to colour it a delicate yellow – rice pilaf. Its name comes from the Arabic word *kurkum*, which means 'saffron', but the two should not be confused. Saffron (page 48) is much more expensive and has a different flavour altogether. Turmeric is the flavouring used for Worcestershire sauce as well as the mustard relish piccalilli.

Turmeric is a relative of ginger. Like ginger, the spice is obtained from the roots, which are a brilliant orange, and harvested and processed in the same way. Turmeric is always traded whole and ground in the consuming country. The roots are boiled, dried, peeled and then ground to produce the bright yellow spice that is used to flavour curries and colour mustards, butter cheeses, drinks and pickles.

Medicinal Uses

Taken internally turmeric is thought to be good for digestive upsets and skin disorders. It is said to improve poor circulation and ease menstrual problems, and is used in Indian herbal medicine for treating liver disorders, uterine tumours and jaundice. It is a strong stimulant of the digestive and respiratory systems and also has anti-inflammatory and antiseptic properties. Externally, turmeric can be applied in a poultice to sores and wounds and can be used for ringworm.

Storage

Turmeric is almost alw as a ground powder be the root is very hard t Only small quantities be bought because it flavour, but not its c very quickly.

Ground turmeric has such a strong colour it is used for colouring as much as for flavour.

Lemongrass
Cymbopogon citratus

Although lemongrass is a relatively new spice to the West, it should now be available in most supermarkets. Asian markets sell both fresh and dry lemongrass, sometimes under the Indonesian name *sereh*. Its rich lemony flavour and fragrance make it a tangy, spicy addition to many foods. It is a principal ingredient in Thai, Malaysian and Indonesian cooking and curries.

Origins & Characteristics
lemongrass comes from
Southeast Asia and is a tender
perennial tropical grass, which
grow nearly 2m (6ft) tall.
densely tufted with long,
leaves that, when crushed,
extremely fragrant – this
gives it its name.
flowers are greenish with
orange, and they appear
is in summer.
would try growing
s yourself – the plant
temperature of at least
F), so that may mean
a greenhouse. The
n they are crushed,
tful fragrance to
erfumes.

...s
talks can be
the leaves, once
used in the same
onions to flavour
s and curries.
ould be finely
lded just before
o that it doesn't

e leaves is used
a curry-like
outheast Asian

cooking, especially, with fish and
meat. You can make an infusion
of the dried leaves to be drunk
as an herbal tea. And the finely
chopped fresh leaves can be
floated on summer drinks.

Cosmetic Uses
Lemongrass is used extensively
in the manufacture of oils that
are used in making scented
soaps. This is because it contains
a semidrying property that is
excellent for cleansing oily skin.

Storage
The essential oil produced from
lemongrass (citral) loses its
effectiveness if it is stored in the
light, so it should be kept in a
dark cupboard. It will not store
for very long, so it should be
bought and used fresh.

Medicinal Uses
Lemongrass is taken internally as
a digestive aid for small children
and is also used for mild feverish
complaints. It is a valuable
insecticide and works well
externally as a remedy against
ringworm, scabies and lice. It is
also believed to be an effective
treatment for athlete's foot.

*Lemongrass stalks and leaves can
be used as an insecticide to combat
infestations of lice or ringworm.*

Cardamom
Elettaria cardamomum

There are several varieties of cardamom, each related to ginger and each having a slightly different flavour, but the most common and widely used variety is grown in southern India. Cardamom is both one of the oldest and also highly valued spices in the world – it is the most expensive spice after saffron and vanilla. The Normans brought cardamom to Britain in the eleventh century, and it was very popular in medieval and Tudor recipes. Cardamom is mainly used to flavour curries.

Origins & Characteristics

The best cardamom comes from the rain forests of Malabar, where it grows as a shrub about 2m (6ft) tall, with blue-streaked flowers with yellow tips. It also grows wild throughout India in the tropical mountain forests. It is cultivated in Sri Lanka and Thailand as well as in Central America.

Culinary Uses

In addition to its use in curries, cardamom is used to flavour sausages, breads, cakes and pastries. In the Arab world it is added to coffee as a sign of hospitality because it is one of the most expensive spices – there is also some evidence that it reduces or eliminates the effect of the caffeine in coffee.

In northern Europe, especially the Scandinavian countries, cardamom is used mostly as a flavouring for breads and cakes and as a pickling spice, while in Asia it is used as a hot spice for curries, and the whole pods are used as a vegetable.

Medicinal Uses

Cardamom taken internally may settle upset stomachs and counteract the effects of dairy product allergies. Its warmth is believed to help respiratory disorders, and it is used to revitalise the kidneys.

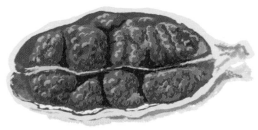

Inside a cardamom pod are the individual seeds.

Storage

Cardamom loses its flavour very quickly, so only very small quantities should be bought. When it is fresh or freshly ground it has a eucalyptus aroma that quickly fades – that is how you can tell if it is fresh. If you buy ground cardamom and it smells of camphor you have been sold a cheap substitute.

It is best to buy the whole pods and grind them yourself rather than to buy it already ground. It loses its flavour so quickly when ground that it will already have deteriorated before it can be sold.

Buy cardamom as pods and grind them yourself; they will keep for longer than the powder.

Cloves
Eugenia caryophyllus

The name 'clove' comes from the Latin word *clavus*, meaning 'nail', which describes its shape. Cloves are the dried flower buds of the clove tree, which is a relative of myrtle. Cloves became known to Europeans by the fourth century as they passed along the spice routes from the East. The Romans and Greeks used cloves extensively in herbal remedies, and there is evidence that cloves were one of the earliest plants used in Chinese herbal medicine.

Origins & Characteristics
The clove tree originally came from the Molucca Islands, but cloves are now cultivated in the West Indies, Zanzibar and Madagascar.

The tree is an evergreen with bright red flowers. It grows very tall – more than 15m (50ft). The flower buds are dried and they turn reddish brown. The dried cloves can be used whole or ground, and the taste is extremely strong – pungent and aromatic – so they need to be used sparingly.

Culinary Uses
Clove is one of the spices used in garam masala, and it can be used to flavour curries, stocks, sauces, pickles, mulled wine, apple dishes, spiced cakes, mincemeat and marinades for meat and fish dishes. It is a very versatile spice and can be used as an ingredient in sauces as well as to flavour fruit punches.

Other Uses
Cloves can be used to give a room a pleasant aroma. Stick several in an orange and hang it up. Cloves also repel insects, so a spoonful tied in a muslin bag can be used in your wardrobe instead of mothballs.

Orange-and-clove pomanders make wonderful aromatic decorations, particularly at Christmas. Pierce the orange with the cloves, pushing them in place in quarter segments of the orange. Dip the orange into a bowl of mixed spices, then cover and leave in a dark cool place for a few days, so that the pomander will draw in the fragrance.

It's easy to see how cloves got their name – from the latin word for nail.

Storage

Fresh cloves should ooze oil if you press the stalk with a fingernail. Because they are so aromatic, they should be kept tightly sealed in lidded glass jars. And remember that you need very few of them – only half a dozen in an apple pie will be enough to flavour it.

Medicinal Uses

A whole clove clamped between the teeth is said to relieve toothache. Cloves are also useful for stimulating the digestive system as they are a warming stimulant. They can be taken internally to treat gastroenteritis, nausea, gastric upsets and impotence.

Cloves will grow hard as they grow stale. If no oil comes out when you squeeze the stalk with your nail, the clove is no longer fresh.

Asafetida
Ferula assafoetida

Asafetida is an Asiatic spice that may be known more commonly in the West as devil's dung, or stinking gum. It is hardly surprising, therefore, that it is little known outside India. The name derives from the Persian word *aza*, meaning 'resin', and the Latin word *fetida*, meaning 'stinking'. It is a resin collected from a perennial plant that grows wild in Afghanistan and eastern Iran. The resin hardens and is sold in lumps, which are ground to a powder and added to vegetables as a delicious flavouring. It also goes well with fish – fresh or salted.

Origins & Characteristics
The plant grows around 2.5m (8ft) tall and is quite foul-smelling, with thick roots. It carries pale yellow-green flowers. The stems are thick and when cut to the root, the milky sap that flows out is collected as a resin, which then hardens.

Although the plant looks like a giant fennel, it is unrelated. In Iran and Afghanistan the leaves and stems are cooked as a vegetable. The smell, caused by sulphurous compounds in the plant, disappears on boiling.

Culinary Uses
Asafetida is mainly used in vegetarian curries, but it can also be used to flavour gravies and stews. The merest pinch added to any fish dish seems to bring out the flavour of the fish and adds an interesting flavour of its own. A little can also be added to relishes.

To use asafetida, the resin needs to be ground into a powder.

Storage

The ground resin is bright yellow and has a truffle-like flavour when cooked. The ground powder has an unpleasant, strong, garlicky odor and should only be used in minute quantities. Naturally, it should be kept quite separate from other spices in airtight, screw-topped glass jars, or its smell will dominate the aromas of other spices and ingredients.

Medicinal Uses

Asafetida is believed to clean and restore the digestive tract and to relieve colic and stomach pains. It is considered a useful treatment for flatulence, constipation and dysentery.

It is said to encourage coughing and, in the East, is given as a remedy for whooping cough and bronchitis. It is sometimes given raw – in pill form to disguise the taste – as an antispasmodic and expectorant.

Asafetida is a hard resin, collected from the Ferula assafoetida *plant.*

Fennel
Foeniculum vulgare

There are several different types of fennel – from Florence fennel to the sweet fennel – but they are all similar in taste and characteristics, and all of them can be grown in your garden. The leaves of the plant are feathery, making it a decorative addition to the border. The Roman (or vulgar fennel), which tastes like aniseed, has been known for thousands of years as a healing and culinary herb, and the Romans used the shoots as a vegetable, but it is the seeds that make an interesting and tasty spice.

Origins & Characteristics

Because fennel grows wild in so many temperate places, it's difficult to say where it originated. It was known and used by the ancient Chinese, Romans, Greeks, Britons, Indians, Egyptians and Persians. They all used the young shoots as a vegetable, dried and ground the seeds as a spice, dried the leaves for tea and used them fresh as a salad. It was used as a remedy for sore eyes, a charm against witchcraft and as an antidote for snake bites. Fennel oil was used as a laxative and as a rub for bronchial congestion.

Culinary Uses

The leaf bases taste like aniseed and can be added to salads. The seeds, dried and bruised, can be used to make a refreshing tea or can be added to fish dishes. The seeds are often sprinkled on the top of bread and cakes.

The stems can be dried and chopped and put inside a roasting chicken for flavour. Alternatively, fennel baked on its own is delicious. Fennel seeds are very warming and can be added to winter stews. You can also finely chop the leaves and add them to yogurt or hummus as an alternative to mint.

Medicinal Uses

Culpeper, the seventeenth century English herbalist, says that the leaves or seed 'boiled in barley water are good for [nursing mothers] to increase the milk, and make it more wholesome for the child'. Fennel is thought to relieve digestive disorders and reduce inflammation. It can be used as a mouthwash and gargle for sore throats.

Tea made from fennel seeds can relax and soothe.

Spicy Herb Tea

You will need:
- 1 tbsp fresh fennel seeds, crushed
- 250ml (9fl oz) hot water
- honey

Add the seeds to the water and leave to steep for five minutes. Sweeten with a little honey and drink while still hot. For colic and to settle upset stomachs, make a decoction by boiling 1½ tsp of fresh crushed seeds in 250ml (9fl oz) of milk.

The leaves, stems and base of fennel are all used in cooking.

Licorice
Glycyrrhiza glabra

Licorice grows widely in the Mediterranean and all the way to China. Its name means 'sweet root', and it is cultivated for its flavour and medicinal properties throughout Europe, especially in Italy. It was once used as a cooking sweetener because it has 50 times the sweetening power of ordinary sugar, but since the advent of sugar plantations, it has fallen out of favour and is now regarded mostly as a weed. This is a shame, because it still has a valuable role to play in cooking and medicine.

Origins & Characteristics

The extremely individual flavour of licorice comes from the root, which is harvested, boiled and filtered and from which the juice is extracted. As it cools, it solidifies into a black, sticky cake. The best of these cakes were always said to be made in Pontefract in northern England, where they still make licorice-flavoured sweets known as Pontefract cakes.

Culinary Uses

Licorice can be used to add a very strong flavour to beers and liqueurs, or it can be added to pipe tobacco to give it an unusual flavour. Its most common use is as a sweet for children.

You can buy commercially produced licorice in its sticky black cake form or as a fresh rhizome (the underground stem of the plant). You could always try to grow your own and harvest the root yourself.

Medicinal Uses

Licorice has a surprising number of uses as a medicinal plant. The dried licorice root or the black extract is used as a vehicle and diluting agent. The root can be chewed or sucked to relieve sore throats and ease other cold symptoms. Licorice is also said to reduce inflammation and spasms, and it is soothing for the lungs because it can expel phlegm and soothe the bronchials.

If you suffer from indigestion, try licorice; it is also used for treating heartburn and is a gentle, natural laxative. In addition, it may lower blood cholesterol and relieve stomach ulcers. Because of its pleasant, sweet taste, licorice is often added to cough mixtures to mask the bitter taste of some of the other ingredients.

Caution
Under some circumstances
licorice can lead to a rise in blood
pressure, so its use should be kept
to a minimum if you have high
blood pressure. Avoid licorice if
you are pregnant.

Sticky black licorice is extracted
from the roots, but you can
also chew on the dried roots
themselves to find relief from
a cold or sore throat.

Star Anise
Illicium verum

One of the most instantly recognisable spices, it is easy to see how star anise gets its name – the shape of the fruit is that of an eight-pointed star. Although unrelated to aniseed (page 88), its essential oil is virtually the same, so both plants have the same aroma. Star anise is the fruit of an evergreen tree that originated in the East Indies but is now cultivated widely in China, where it is used as a food seasoning and in Chinese herbal medicine. In the West it is often added to fish stews. Its essential oil, which is known as oil of aniseed, is used to flavour liqueurs such as pastis in Italy, Germany and France. Its beautiful shape makes it a welcome addition to pot pourris and many decorative projects.

Origins & Characteristics
Star anise is related to the magnolia. The fruits have eight brown seeds and are first harvested when the tree is six years old. By the tree's fifteenth year, it is capable of being cropped three times in a single year, and it continues to be fruitful for many years.

Culinary Uses
The Chinese use star anise in many savoury dishes, especially duck and pork recipes, and they often add the ground seeds to coffee and tea to enhance their flavour. The oil is used to flavour drinks. If you need a strong aniseed flavour in cooking, it is even better to use star anise than aniseed.

Other Uses
The bark can be ground and used as an incense. The Japanese star anise (*Illicium religiosum*) is regarded as a sacred plant, and the tree, which is smaller than star anise, is often planted around temples and near graves. The seeds of star anise can be chewed to sweeten the breath.

Medicinal Uses
Star anise is a diuretic and appetite stimulant and is also used for relieving flatulence and nausea. In Chinese herbal medicine it is recommended for lumbago, constipation, bladder problems, relieving colic and easing the symptoms of acute rheumatism. It is also used to flavour cough medicines.

Storage
Keep the seeds in a screw-topped
glass jar to preserve their flavour.
You will find the spicy, sweet
taste is stronger than anise.

Caution
Do not confuse with Japanese
star anise (*Illicium religiosum*),
the fruit of which is poisonous.
You can tell the difference by the
smells: Japanese star anise smells
like turpentine.

*Star anise seeds are carried
within the star-shaped flowers.*

Elecampane flowers look like small sunflowers, but to encourage strong root growth you need to sacrifice the blooms.

Elecampane
Inula helenium

Origins & Characteristics
Native to central Asia, elecampane was said to have sprung from the tears of Helen of Troy – hence its Latin name. The rayed yellow flowers look like small sunflowers, and it is a tall, rather attractive plant with oval, downy leaves.

Culinary Uses
The flower stems must be removed to encourage root growth, and the roots are harvested after two years, when they are scraped and dried in the sun. They then have a strong, bitter, warm taste. The leaves can be added to salads or used to make a tea that stimulates the appetite. The roots can be boiled in water, sliced and used in salads.

Elecampane is used to flavour liqueurs such as vermouth. It can also be candied to be eaten as a sweet. The leaves can be dried and used to make an herbal tea that is said to be good for stimulating the appetite in invalids and sickly children.

You can steep the root in wine to make a pleasant cordial drink that is said to cause mirth.

Medicinal Uses
Elecampane's warming qualities may make it useful as an expectorant to treat bronchitis, asthma and other pulmonary infections. When applied

This delightfully pretty wild plant grows anywhere in temperate climates that can provide places with the dampness it likes, especially ditches and wet fields, where it can be found in abundance. It is also known as wild sunflower (because of its flowers' similarity to the larger plant), scabwort and horseheal – the latter two names give some indication of its healing properties when applied externally. It is cultivated widely in the Balkan peninsula.

externally as a poultice, the leaves are said to cure scabies, herpes and other skin disorders. It has long been used as a treatment for horse wounds and sores.

The plant is also said to help bring on menstruation and to treat anemia. Soak 3½ tsp of the dried root in 1l (1¾ pints) of water overnight, then boil for 30 minutes and allow to cool. A small cupful three times a day is said to aid digestion. This mixture can also be used as a gargle and mouthwash. You can also chew the fresh root raw as a breath freshener.

Juniper
Juniperus communis

There are many different forms of juniper – from the common juniper to the red cedars of North America. Some, such as the common juniper, are used medicinally and in cooking, while others such as *Juniperus sabina* contain an oil – podophyllotoxin – that is considered too poisonous to use. Juniper has long been considered a magic plant that wards off evil and bad spirits. It was often burned in rooms occupied by the sick, both to fumigate the air and to drive out the demons. Nowadays it is well known as the spice that flavours gin and other cordials. Juniper berries can be gathered in the wild.

Origins & Characteristics
Juniper is widespread throughout the world. It grows as a small evergreen shrub or a tree of only about 3m (9ft) tall. It carries cones, the females of which turn into berries. The berries start off green and slowly turn black over a three-year period, which is how long they take to ripen.

Culinary Uses
The Latin word *Juniperus* comes from the Dutch word *genever*, which gave us the word 'gin'. And that is one of the best uses for juniper – flavouring gin. Dried juniper berries are added to pâtés, game, venison and marinades. They will add flavour to potatoes, sauerkraut, sausages and casseroles. Traditionally they have been used with game because they help to remove some of the stronger 'gamey' taste, which some people do not like. Fresh berries are used to make a conserve to accompany cold meats. The leaves can be used fresh or dried with grilled fish, and the wood and leaves can be used on a barbecue to give a subtle flavour to meat.

Medicinal Uses
Juniper is used for urinary tract infections as well as to treat gout and rheumatism.

It can stimulate the uterus and reduce inflammation of the digestive system.

Caution
Avoid juniper if you are pregnant.

🍲 JUNIPER CONSERVE

You will need:
- juniper berries
- sugar

Cover the berries with water and cook until soft. Drain, then crush the pulp and add sugar to the equivalent of three times the weight of the pulp. Beat vigorously and let cool and set.

Juniper berries have a wide range of medicinal and culinary uses and can often be gathered wild from hedgerows.

The Murrya koenigii *plant needs a tropical environment to grow.*

Curry Leaf
Murrya koenigii

Origins & Characteristics

Curry leaf grows only in tropical regions, so it is not really suited to temperate climates unless it is grown in a greenhouse. Curry plants (*Helichrysum angustifolium*) will grow in any moderate, well-drained soil as long as they get full sun.

Culinary Uses

Curry leaves should be added fresh to curries and spicy meat dishes. The leaves look like bay leaves. They are the essential ingredient in Madras curry powder and give it its unique aroma and flavour. The leaves should be removed before serving. The dried leaves have almost no flavour, but the powdered leaves can sometimes be bought in shops specialising in Indian food. Good storage preserves its flavour.

Curry leaves should be added to dishes as a fresh sprig. They are excellent for steamed vegetables to give them a faint curry flavour. They can also be used to flavour rice, soups and stews. The sprig should be removed before it is served. Curry plants give off a very strong aroma of curry.

Add curry leaves whole to dishes when cooking, so that they can easily be removed before serving.

In India and Sri Lanka, curry leaf is added to curries to strengthen their curry flavour, and it is grown throughout Asia for this purpose; the fresh leaves are widely available. Curry leaves come from a small, ornamental tree that grows wild in the Himalayan foothills. In the West only dried leaves are commercially supplied, and by the time they arrive, they have lost most, if not all, of their flavour. However, there is a Western equivalent, although it is a completely different plant – the curry plant *Helichrysum angustifolium*. This is also used as a tea in Africa – Hottentot tea.

Other Uses

Curry plants can be used to give pot pourri an aromatic and spicy aroma. *Helichrysum angustifolium* has a relative, *H. bracteatum*, which is known as an everlasting flower. Its pretty petals will add colour to any flower arrangement. It can also be used for garlands and wreaths.

Medicinal Uses

The bark of curry leaf is used internally for digestive problems, and the leaves are used as an infusion for constipation and colic. The curry plant, *Helichrysum angustifolium*, has little value as a medicinal plant.

Mace
Myristica fragrans

Mace is the bright red, shiny fiber that covers the nutmeg seed inside the fruit of the nutmeg tree. It is a web-like form of flesh that, when dried, becomes brittle and turns from red to brownish yellow. Nutmeg (page 76) and mace, though they come from the same tree, have different aromas, tastes and uses and should be regarded as two separate spices. Indonesian mace is usually orange-red; mace from Grenada is orange-yellow.

Origins & Characteristics

The fruits of the nutmeg tree are not unlike apricots. The tree is believed to have originated in the Molucca Islands of the East Indies, but it is now cultivated in many countries, such as Indonesia, Brazil, Sri Lanka and the West Indies.

The Arabs spread the use of mace throughout the Arab world and subsequently all over Europe. During Tudor times in England it was used a lot and considered one of the finest, if not most expensive, spices available.

When the Dutch East India Company controlled most of the world's spice trade during the seventeenth and eighteenth centuries, there was a story about how an official in the head office in Amsterdam sent a request to the governor of the Far Eastern colonies to grow fewer nutmegs and more mace because they got more revenue from mace – nutmeg being considered an inferior spice. He didn't realise that they came from the same tree.

Culinary Uses

Nutmeg and mace are used the most extensively by Europeans, both in sweet and savoury meals. Unlike nutmeg, which is mainly used as a sweet spice, mace is a strong and aromatic savoury spice best suited to baked fish, bechamel sauces, beef stews, casseroles and to season vegetables and potatoes. It should be added just before serving; a little can be grated over the top of any dish.

Unlike the related nutmeg, mace has a strong and savoury flavour.

Storage

Mace in its whole form is known as blades of mace and loses its flavour quite quickly; however, it is fairly pungent and should be kept separate from other spices or it will taint them. It should be kept in a tightly lidded glass jar.

Medicinal Uses

Mace is used to treat stomach disorders such as diarrhoea, dysentery and indigestion.

Mace is the fibrous red 'skin' that surrounds a nutmeg. They may come from the same plant, but the two spices are used in quite different ways.

Nutmeg
Myristica fragrans

The inner seed of the nutmeg tree, lying inside the filigree covering of mace (page 74), is the nutmeg. A nutmeg is quite large – about 1.5cm (½in) long – and extremely hard. For this reason they are never used whole, but always grated. Once the seed has been separated from the mace, it is left to dry. It can then be grated in very small quantities into hot spicy drinks and used to flavour and sweeten desserts with its warm and highly aromatic taste.

Origins & Characteristics
Nutmeg trees grow in hot, tropical places and are extremely difficult to grow. The nutmeg has always been cheaper to produce than mace because it requires little processing before it can be sold, whereas mace has to be dried carefully to prevent decay. The oil of small or damaged nutmeg seeds is extracted and used in the cosmetic industry.

Culinary Uses
You can grate nutmeg over puddings, custards and ice cream, as well as use it to flavour hot spicy drinks such as mulled wine. It is a flavourful addition to stewed fruit such as apples and pears and is used in baking spicy cakes and biscuits.

Medicinal Uses
In India, nutmeg was used as a cure for headaches, insomnia and urinary incontinence. In small doses nutmeg is carminative and is used in treating flatulence and vomiting and for improving overall digestion.

Storage
Nutmeg is its own best storage container. Whole spices will keep for three or four years. Small quantities can be grated from the whole nutmeg when needed. They should be stored in lidded glass jars.

Other Uses
Nutmeg oil is used in the cosmetic industry in soaps, shampoos and perfumes.

Caution
Nutmeg contains myristicin, which is a hallucinatory compound and should be regarded as a potential poison. As little as two whole nutmegs could be enough to cause death.

🫕 BAKED BANANA CUSTARD WITH NUTMEG

You will need:
- 6 ripe bananas
- 75g (3oz) light brown demerara sugar
- 1 tsp nutmeg, grated
- 1 tbsp lime juice
- 500ml (18fl oz) egg custard
- 50g (2oz) breadcrumbs

Mash the bananas and mix with the sugar, nutmeg and lime juice. Place in buttered dish. Cover with breadcrumbs and add a layer of egg custard. Sprinkle with a little nutmeg and bake at 175°C (350°F) for 35 minutes or until golden brown on top.

Nutmeg keeps longest in its whole form (right), so just grate it in small quantities as you need it (left).

Myrtle
Myrtus communis

Myrtle has long been considered a plant of love – it is named after Myrrha, a favourite priestess of Venus. It is said that Venus transformed Myrrha into the evergreen shrub to protect her from the unwelcome attentions of a suitor. When Paris gave Venus the golden apple for beauty, she was wearing a wreath of myrtle and even today it is still often woven into bridal wreaths. An Arabic story tells of how Adam gave Eve a sprig of myrtle to declare his love – and she gave him an apple.

Origins & Characteristics

Myrtle is an evergreen shrub that grows quite tall – up to 5m (16ft) – with glossy leaves that are quite aromatic. The flowers are cream-coloured and give way to blue-black berries.

In the wild, myrtle grows in dry, hilly conditions in North Africa, southern Europe and the Middle East. The fruits are known as mursins. The flowers can be dried for pot pourri, and the leaves and fruit can be used either fresh or dried as an aromatic spicy flavouring for game and roasted meats.

Culinary Uses

The branches and leaves, burned on a grill, give meat a delicate, spicy flavour. You can use the fresh leaves to stuff game birds and the dried leaves to flavour stews and casseroles. The fruit, dried and ground, can be added to any savoury dish. The flavour is quite sweet but spicy – not unlike juniper berries (page 70).

Medicinal Uses

Myrtle is a carminative and expectorant and is thought to be helpful in cases of chest infections. The oil is extracted and used to treat acne.

In China, the dried and powdered leaves were used as an astringent dusting powder for babies when they were wrapped in swaddling clothes.

For a tea that may relieve psoriasis and sinusitis, infuse the myrtle leaf – you may need to add honey for taste. A cold compress of the leaves can be used for bruises and haemorrhoids.

Glossy leaves and blue-black
berries make myrtle a striking
plant. Scatter some leaves over
your barbecue coals to add
flavour to the meat.

Nigella seeds are only very small, but have an interesting angular shape. Only seeds from Nigella sativa (above) should be used for flavouring food; other varieties have cosmetic uses.

Nigella
Nigella sativa

Origins & Characteristics

Nigella grows wild throughout the whole of Asia and the Middle East, where it has traditionally been used in the same way in which we use black pepper today. In India, where the seeds are called *kalonji*, they are used as a pickling spice. In the Bible they are referred to as 'fitches', from the Hebrew word *ketzah*, meaning 'vetch'.

There are 14 different varieties in the *Nigella* genus, including love-in-a-mist, and they are mostly grown for their use in dried flower arrangements.

Culinary Uses

You can use the seeds to flavour curries, meat dishes, chutneys, pickles, sauces and cooked vegetables. The Bengalis use them as a flavouring for fish dishes. The seeds can be ground in a pepper mill and used in the same way you would use black pepper. The seeds can be added to breads and pastries to give a little pungency. Because the seeds do have an irritant effect, they should be used sparingly.

Medicinal Uses

Traditionally nigella was given to nursing mothers to increase milk production and to help the uterus recover. The seeds are said to benefit digestion and reduce inflammation or irritation in the stomach lining.

Nigella is known by many other names including nutmeg flower, black cumin, Roman coriander and fennel flower, and is the common name for a particular variety within the *Nigella* family – *Nigella sativus*. The seeds of this pretty, annual herbaceous plant are black and can be dried and ground to provide a fruity tasting spice. It is often confused with the related plant, *Nigella damascena* (love-in-a-mist). The two plants are very similar but only *Nigella sativa* should be used as a spice. The seeds of love-in-a-mist are distilled for an essential oil used in perfumes and lipsticks. The flowers of *Nigella sativa* are small and white with a blue tinge.

Growing

Nigella damascena (love-in-a-mist) is easy to grow and makes a good flower for dried arrangements (though it is very invasive in borders). *Nigella sativa* needs more sun and well-drained soil. Sow seeds in the autumn or spring and do not try to transplant. Do not grow both varieties as they will cross-pollinate.

Nigella seeds are traditionally used to stimulate milk production in breastfeeding mothers.

Poppy
Papaver somniferum

The tiny blue-black seeds of the lilac-coloured opium poppy, as it is commonly called, were used as a spice by the Sumerians as long ago as 4000 B.C. Nowadays it is cultivated in many countries both for its use as a culinary spice and for its medicinal qualities – it is used to make morphine and codeine.

Origins & Characteristics

Opium poppies grow wild in the Middle East; and they were first taken to China a thousand years ago. They were used for their pain-relieving properties in ancient Greece, Egypt and Italy, as well as India and the Middle Eastern countries. Opium is obtained from the flesh of the unripe seed heads – the seeds themselves do not contain any of the drug. The plant grows around 1.2m (4ft) tall: twice as tall as the bright red corn, or field, poppy of Europe (*Papaver rhoeas*). The opium poppy also has a variety with white flowers.

Culinary Uses

In Middle Eastern cooking the seeds are used to flavour sweet dishes and to make cakes, puddings and strudel fillings. In India, which produces an opium poppy with yellow seeds, the seeds are called *khas khas* and are used to flavour meat dishes. In most European countries the seeds are sprinkled onto newly baked bread to impart a nutty flavour. There is a Jewish three-cornered pastry called *hamantaschen*, which has a filling completely made of poppy seeds. You can try making cakes of poppy seeds with honey – it is said that they were given to the athletes of ancient Greece for extra energy before they took part in the Olympics.

Medicinal Uses

Opium poppy seeds are used for treating cystitis and pyelitis; make an infusion and add honey to sweeten the taste.

Caution

In some countries there may be a legal restriction on growing opium poppies; all parts of the plant, except the seeds, are poisonous. The seeds should not be given to anyone suffering from hay fever or from any other allergic condition.

Poppy seeds can be collected from the dried flowerheads.

🍲 NOODLES WITH POPPY SEED

You will need:
- 200g (8oz) noodles
- 10g (⅓oz) unsalted butter
- 2 tsp poppy seeds
- salt and black pepper

Cook the noodles and add unsalted butter, poppy seeds, and salt and pepper to taste. Stir well and eat. This works well as a side dish with a rich meat stew like goulash.

The opium poppy has been grown as a spice for many thousands of years.

Quassia
Picraena excelsa

This spice is also known as Jamaican quassia or bitter ash. It is similar and closely related to Japanese quassia (*Picraena ailanthoides*) and Surinam quassia (*Quassia amara*). They are all deciduous trees from tropical America, India or Malaysia. The word 'quassia' describes the bitter compound extracted from the wood and bark; at one time brewers used it instead of hops to flavour beer.

Origins & Characteristics
The quassia tree grows very tall – over 25m (80ft) – and looks a little like the ash tree. It has small, pale-yellow flowers. The wood is used in the form of chips, which are used to flavour tonic wines and beers. If you fill wooden cups made from this tree with water and leave them to stand overnight, you will have a bitter drink that is said to be good for stimulating the flow of gastric juices in the stomach and sharpening the appetite.

Medicinal Uses
Only small doses of quassia should be taken for general revitalisation. Quassia is also used to treat rheumatism and fevers, stomach disorders and dyspepsia. A tea made from the wood chips is said to be a cure for alcoholism, and an infusion used as a shampoo is said to clear up dandruff. It can also be taken internally as a tea to kill roundworms.

Culinary Uses
Quassia chips have an intensely bitter taste but no smell. When added to water or alcohol, they produce a yellow colour. Quassia is used in the production of bitters, which were traditionally used in the spring to increase the secretions of digestive juices and stimulate sluggish stomachs, thus restoring the appetite – especially important after a winter of heavily salted and stodgy food.

Quassia is used as a spice in its wood chip form; it is bitter, but said to stimulate digestion.

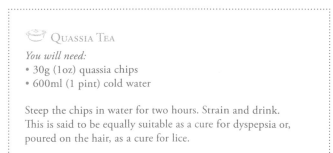

🫖 QUASSIA TEA

You will need:
- 30g (1oz) quassia chips
- 600ml (1 pint) cold water

Steep the chips in water for two hours. Strain and drink.
This is said to be equally suitable as a cure for dyspepsia or,
poured on the hair, as a cure for lice.

*The quassia is a very large tree
with delicate yellow blooms.*

Allspice
Pimento officinalis

Allspice is also known as Jamaican pepper and pimento – itself another name for a type of red pepper. None of its names is really helpful – it is not a spice combination and it is not a pepper. Moreover, 'pimento' is a word that was used during the Middle Ages to describe any spice. 'Allspice' is the name given to this aromatic spice by John Ray (1627–1705), an English botanist who thought it tasted like a combination of cinnamon, nutmeg and cloves. It is said to have first been brought back to Europe from its native Jamaica by Christopher Columbus and is still cultivated in Jamaica on plantations known as pimento walks.

Origins & Characteristics
Allspice is the dried fruit of a tree that is native to Central and South America. The flowers are small and white, and the fruits are gathered unripe and dried in the hot sun until they turn a reddish brown. The tree can grow to an enormous height – over 15m (50ft).

Culinary Uses
Allspice should be bought whole and ground as needed. You can use it in much the same way you would use any of the three flavours it resembles – in hot spicy drinks and mulled wine; as a pickling spice; or for puddings and custards. It can also be used for meat and fish dishes to which it gives an unusual and spicy flavour. It's especially good with lamb – some say it tastes of juniper berries (page 70). The leaves are used to make bay rum, and the flowers can be infused for a tea. You can add it as a powder to curry dishes and use it to flavour shellfish.

If you can buy the whole berries, you can grind your own – or try adding a couple to your pepper mill to add a little zest to your black pepper.

Medicinal Uses
The oil is distilled and used for flatulent indigestion. It improves the overall digestion and is said to have a tonic effect on the nervous system.

Cosmetic Uses
You can grate a little allspice into your bath water as an antiseptic and anaesthetic – as well as for its beautiful aroma.

Allspice earned its name because it was thought to taste like several different spices.

The black fruits of the allspice tree (above) are gathered before they fully ripen and are dried before use (left).

Aniseed (Anise)
Pimpinella anisum

The oval-shaped, aromatic seeds of *Pimpinella anisum* are one of the world's oldest known spices. The ancient Romans were the first to really discover and use the pungent and spicy aniseed to flavour their cakes, which they ate after heavy meals to settle their stomachs. Anise, as it is also called, is the flavour in the popular Greek drink ouzo.

Origins & Characteristics

Aniseed grows wild throughout the Middle East, but it can also be cultivated in any moderately warm climate. It grows to about 45cm (18in) tall, with broadish leaves and small cream-coloured flowers that give way to tiny, light-brown hairy seeds. It was first cultivated by the ancient Egyptians and then spread throughout the Arab, Roman and Greek worlds. It has been grown commercially for a very long time but is now being slowly replaced by *Illicium verum* – star anise (page 66) because it is cheaper to grow.

Culinary Uses

The fresh leaves can be used to flavour curries and spicy meat dishes, while the seeds can be chewed to sweeten the breath afterwards. The taste is similar to fennel – sweet and spicy – although the leaves have a more delicate flavour. It is used to flavour sweets that young children love. And it is also used to flavour various liqueurs such as ouzo, pastis and arak.

Medicinal Use

Aniseed has warming and stimulating properties and it is these properties that make it useful for treating circulation problems and digestive disorders. It is also soothing for the lungs as an expectorant and is used to both flavour and activate cough medicines. More mysteriously, it is said to avert the evil eye. The oil is used in the production of toothpaste, and aniseed tea is used for settling indigestion and improving overall digestion.

Tiny aniseed seeds have a powerful flavour.

🍲 ANISEED CAKES

You will need:
- 3 medium eggs
- 100g (4oz) light brown demerara sugar
- 150g (6oz) whole wheat flour
- 2 tsp aniseed powder
- 1 tsp baking powder

Beat the eggs, add the sugar and beat for three more minutes. Mix the dry ingredients together and fold into the beaten eggs and sugar. Drop a spoonful of the mixture into each depression of a cupcake tray and let stand for 12 hours. Bake at 160°C (325°F) for 12 minutes or until the cakes brown nicely. Eat while they are still hot, spread with a little honey for total indulgence.

The leaves and seeds of aniseed are both used for flavouring and for medicinal remedies.

Cubeb
Piper cubeba

Cubeb is an unusual and very hot spice grown in Sumatra, Penang and New Guinea. It is also known as Java pepper, tailed pepper and tailed cubebs. It is the unripe fruit of a climbing pepper plant that grows like a vine. The dried unripe berries are used and they look the same as the dried berries of black pepper (page 92) – both come from the same family and are closely related. Cubeb berries come with little tails attached and once dried have a wrinkled leathery appearance. Compared with pepper, cubeb is a lot more fiery and aromatic. It is used a lot in Indonesian cooking. If the berries are split open some will have a small seed inside them while others will be hollow.

Origins & Characteristics

Cubeb likes rich clay soil with high humidity and lots of shade. It grows well in subtropical forests. The fruits are picked unripe and dried for use in powders, tinctures and liquid extracts or distilled for their oleoresin and oil, which are used by manufacturers to flavour sauces, relishes, bitters and even tobacco. The oil is also used in the production of perfumes and toiletries.

Culinary Uses

Cubeb is used widely in Indonesian food as a hot and spicy pepper addition to rice dishes, curries and fish. It has a taste similar to allspice (page 86) and can be used to replace this spice when necessary. Be careful – it can be quite bitter if too much is used.

Medicinal Uses

Because of its warming properties, cubeb is said to relieve coughs and bronchitis, sinusitis and throat infection. Traditionally in Indonesia it was used as an antiseptic against gonorrhoea, but there is no evidence of its effectiveness in this respect.

When the oil is added to tobacco it is said to relieve hay fever, asthma and pharyngitis. An infusion is made by steeping 1 tsp of powdered cubeb in 250ml (9fl oz) of hot water – a mouthful can be taken three times a day to relieve upset stomachs, indigestion and urinary infections.

Cubeb berries have a distinctive appearance, with their wizened skins and little 'tails'.

🍲 Hot Indonesian Rice

You will need:
- 2 onions, finely chopped
- cubeb
- coriander seeds
- cardamom
- turmeric
- 250g (9fl oz) cooked rice, cold
- 3 bananas, as unripe as possible
- 4 eggs

Brown the onions and add the spices – you need to experiment to adjust the quantities to suit your own taste; you could start with ¼ tsp of each and adjust accordingly. Add the rice to the onions and spices. Slice the bananas lengthwise and fry. Cook the eggs quite dry – omelette style – and then slice. Serve the rice on a plate with the bananas and eggs around it.

A warming spice, good for coughs and sore throats, cubeb also adds a hot and peppery flavour to food.

Pepper
Piper nigrum

Black pepper is not related to sweet peppers (page 30), but comes from the climbing vine *Piper nigrum*, which grows in Southeast Asia. The berries are picked unripe and green and left to dry in the sun to produce black peppercorns. Berries that are left to ripen turn red. These are picked and soaked to get rid of the outer dark husk, then the inner peppercorn is dried to become white pepper. The unripe berries pickled in brine are called green pepper, and ripe ones, pink pepper. Pepper has always been a valuable spice – we get the term 'peppercorn rent' from the way pepper was used to pay taxes and rent during the eighteenth century and in Roman times it was the most expensive of all spices.

Origins & Characteristics
Originally a native of the Malabar coast, pepper is now grown in tropical regions throughout the world; mainly in India, the East Indies and Asia. Black pepper has a strong, pungent flavour, while white pepper has a milder flavour but is sharper, hotter and less aromatic. Peppercorns can be bought whole or ground, but ground pepper loses its flavour more quickly.

Culinary Uses
Pepper contains a volatile oil that actually helps in the digestion of meat and high-protein foods by stimulating the digestive juices. There are few savoury dishes that do not benefit from a little black pepper being added to them. White pepper is generally used in pale-coloured dishes in which the use of black pepper would spoil the appearance. Sauces can be made from the whole peppercorn; they are also used in pickling spices, bouquet garni (page 116) and marinades.

Medicinal Uses
Pepper is said to be very good for stimulating the digestion, warming the bronchial passageways and relieving congestion.

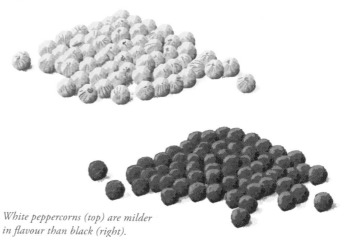

White peppercorns (top) are milder in flavour than black (right).

Unripe berries are picked when they are green (left) and dried to make black pepper; ripe red berries (right) are used for white pepper.

The sumac is a widespread shrub, but some varieties are poisonous. It is not advised to collect fruits in the wild.

Sumac
Rhus coriaria

Origins & Characteristics
Sumac is valued for its high tannin content and its astringent properties. It is related to poison ivy and grows wild as a tall shrub in thickets. The roots are harvested and dried, and the outer bark is stripped off. The fruits are collected when ripe, left to dry and then powdered before use.

Culinary Uses
In Lebanon the dried fruits are used in the same way in which we use lemon juice in cooking – as a souring agent. The seeds are crushed and then steeped in water to extract the juice. You can also buy sumac powder, which you add to savoury dishes to give them a sharpish bite. In Turkey, powdered sumac is commonly added to hummus, both to enhance the flavour and to act as a decoration. The North American native peoples used to make a cordial drink from the fresh red berries.

Medicinal Uses
Sumac is taken internally for treating severe diarrhoea, and the root bark is used to treat dysentery. The fruits are used for treating urinary infections. The root bark is also used externally for treating haemorrhoids. A tea made from the bark or leaves is said to be good as a gargle for sore throats.

There are two distinct types of sumac that can be used as spices – the Middle Eastern variety *Rhus coriaria*, known as Sicilian sumac, and the North American sumac *Rhus aromatica*. Altogether there are more than 250 species of sumac. Some are quite poisonous, so care needs to be taken to make sure the right ones are used. The Chinese sumac *Rhus chinensis* is used widely in herbal medicine for treating coughs and mouth ulcers but has no culinary use. Sumac is not very well known in the West but can be procured from some Middle Eastern shops in its ground form.

The American native peoples made a poultice from the fresh red berries to treat the irritation of poison ivy.

Other Uses
The tree's bark and leaves can be used as a dye.

Caution
Make sure you don't confuse the sumacs – some species are poisonous. Do not use the ornamental sumac.

Sumac powder can be used in cooking to flavour savoury dishes. It is often sprinkled as a garnish over hummus.

Sesame
Sesamum indicum

Origins & Characteristics
Sesame is a native of India, Indonesia, Africa and China; it grows well in sandy soil and needs a hot climate. It is a tall annual with white, trumpet-shaped flowers that turn into seed capsules about 2.5cm (1in) long. They burst open when ripe and have a sweet, nutty flavour when lightly roasted. Some cultivated varieties do not burst, and this makes them easier to harvest.

Culinary Uses
The ground sesame seed is sold as a paste called tahini, which is used in Greek cuisine and is made into *halvah*, a sweetmeat eaten with strong coffee in the Middle East. Sesame seeds are sprinkled over bread and cakes. Toasted sesame seeds can be added to vegetables and cheese sauces and used instead of breadcrumbs on fish pies. Sesame oil is used widely in cooking. Sesame seeds are also an important alternative to nuts for anyone with a nut allergy. They are used commercially in the production of margarine and cooking oils and even in soaps and lubricants.

Sesame seeds (left) are contained in pods that form from the trumpet-shaped white flowers of the plant.

Sesame is a valuable and important addition to any cook's spice cupboard. It is also one of the earliest spices known to have been used both for its seeds and the oil contained in them. It is recorded in use in Egypt around 5,000 years ago, and there is evidence that it was being cultivated commercially in India as far back as 1600 B.C. Sesame was once believed to have magical powers. Ali Baba's famous phrase, 'open sesame', probably springs from the seedpods' tendency to burst open suddenly.

Medicinal Uses
There are few conditions that have not been treated at some time with sesame seeds. This spice can help with hair loss, dysentery, dizziness, headaches, osteoporosis and boils. Because the seeds are very high in calories, they are good for convalescent people. They also make a mild and gentle laxative.

Cosmetic Uses
The oil from sesame seeds is used by Mediterranean women to treat dry skin conditions because it softens and penetrates well. It is also a good suntan oil, because it absorbs most of the ultraviolet rays and is resistant to water, so it will not wash off if you go swimming.

White Mustard
Sinapsis alba

White mustard seeds are larger and much milder than those of the black mustard and are a pale brown or yellow. They are used to make American mustard and mixed with black mustard to make English mustard, but are not used in French mustard. The herbalist Culpeper recommended that white mustard be applied to the soles of the feet in a poultice for fevers and rheumatic and sciatic pains – to act upon the nerves whenever a strong stimulating medicine is wanted and not excite heat. Conversely, Pliny once observed that mustard has so pungent a flavour that it burns like fire. Pliny also noted 40 remedies that were made using mustard.

Origins & Characteristics

White mustard is thought to have originated in the Mediterranean but will grow well in any temperate, dry climate in heavy, sandy soil. It is an annual, growing about 1m (3ft) tall, with yellow flowers that turn into seed pods about 2.5cm (1in) long. The seeds are harvested, dried and ground.

Culinary Uses

White mustard has a pleasant, nutty flavour and is not as hot as black mustard, so it can be used more freely in cooking. The seeds can be used for pickling and can be sprouted with cress to make 'mustard and cress' – because the mustard seeds grow more quickly they should be sown three days later than the cress.

A mustard made with white mustard seeds is quite mild and is traditionally used to accompany American hot dogs and barbecued meat. Use a little grape juice with your mustard powder if you want to reduce its fieriness – use cold water if you want it full strength.

Medicinal Uses

In Chinese medicine white mustard is used to treat bronchial congestion, colds, coughs and rheumatic joint pains.

Caution

Mustard contains substances that can irritate mucous membranes and is also a skin irritant, so home medicinal use should be avoided.

⌣ HERB MUSTARD

You will need:

- 60g (2oz) white mustard seed (use powdered if you can't get the seed)
- ¼ tsp herb pepper
- 60g (2oz) Mignonette pepper
- 7g (⅓oz) thyme
- 7g (⅓oz) marjoram
- ¼ tsp lemon peel
- pinch of dried rosemary
- ¼ tsp orange peel
- 1 tsp honey
- 1 tsp wine or herb vinegar
- pinch of turmeric

Grind the mustard as necessary and add all other ingredients. Mix to a paste and use with cold meats – do not store; consume immediately.

White mustard seeds (opposite) are larger than black mustard and are harvested from seedpods that follow the yellow flowers.

Tamarind
Tamarindus indica

Tamarind is known as the date of India, because it has been cultivated in India for centuries. It is widely used in Asian cooking. It is also used in Africa, Iraq and the countries bordering the Persian Gulf in southwestern Asia, in chutneys, curries and relishes. In Tudor times it was appreciated in England as a refreshing summer cordial, tamarind water, having probably been introduced to Europe by the Crusaders.

Origins & Characteristics

Tamarind grows as a large, dark pod on the tamarind tree, which is a native of tropical eastern Asia. The fruits can be eaten fresh or dried to make a souring agent and used as one would lemon juice. The taste is both sweet and sour, aromatic and spicy. The tamarind tree grows to a height of some 30m (100ft) and can reach more than 10m (30ft) in girth. It is now cultivated in the West Indies and has become an important spice ingredient in Mexican cooking.

Culinary Use

Tamarind can be purchased as a fibrous, black, sticky pulp known as tamarind paste, which is the husk without the seeds. You extract the flavour by soaking it in hot water to which a little sugar has been added, and then squeezing it. It is a useful flavour to add to curries, meat or fish, and it has a stronger taste than either lemon or lime juice. It is also available in a dried and ground form.

Medicinal Uses

Tamarind makes an excellent laxative – its action is quite gentle. It is also used to treat fevers, asthma, jaundice and dysentery. Women who experience morning sickness in early pregnancy can eat the fruit to relieve the nausea. It is also said to increase appetite and aid digestion.

Tamarind is sold as a block of paste (below) – black, sticky and fibrous – or in dried, ground form.

Tamarind Water

You will need:
- 50–70g (2½oz) tamarind paste
- 2l (3½ pints) water
- 3 tbsp sugar
- ½ sliced lemon

Soak the tamarind paste in the water overnight. Strain and add the sugar and lemon. Bring to a boil and simmer for five minutes. Let cool and strain again. This refreshing cordial makes a pleasant cold summer drink. You can add a little fruit or a sprig of mint to serve.

The pods of the tamarind tree contain blackish seeds, that can be dried or used when still fresh.

Fenugreek
Trigonella foenum-graecum

Fenugreek is also known as bird's foot and Greek clover and is grown throughout the world for its medicinal and culinary uses. The seeds have a mild curry flavour and a bitter aftertaste. It is probably best known in the West for its use in the Middle Eastern sweetmeat halva. Because of its ability to restore nitrogen to the soil, fenugreek is used in the East as cattle fodder. It is also unusual for a spice in being a good source of protein.

Origins & Characteristics

Fenugreek was probably first grown and recognised as a useful spice in Assyria some time around the seventh century B.C. It spread to India and China and is now used worldwide. In Egypt it is sold as a dried plant called *hilba* as a remedy for painful menstruation.

The leaves are picked in summer and used fresh or dried in infusions. The seeds are collected and dried to be powdered or used whole. The Egyptians used it as an ingredient in their embalming fluids. In Yemen it is ground to a paste and added to vegetable dishes.

Culinary Uses

In India the dried leaves of fenugreek, called *methi*, are a valuable addition to curries. The seeds can be left to sprout and used as a salad vegetable. The ground seeds are used in chutneys and relishes – mango chutney often has the whole seeds in it. The seeds can be lightly roasted to reduce the bitter aftertaste. In Ethiopia it is used as a condiment and in baking bread. You can use the seeds in fried foods, stews and pastries.

Cosmetic Uses

For an infusion that can be used for washing the face and hair, infuse the seeds by using 2 tsp of seeds steeped in 250ml (9fl oz) of cold water for six hours. Then boil for one minute and let cool. This infusion is said to improve skin condition and hair quality. You can also mix the seeds with oil for a stimulating massage oil.

Fenugreek leaves can be dried to preserve them for longer.

Medicinal Uses

Traditionally fenugreek has been given to men suffering from impotence and to women to bring on childbirth. The seeds can be infused to treat gastric inflammation, colic, insufficient lactation, poor appetite and digestive disorders. In Chinese herbal medicine they are used to treat kidney disorders and oedema.

Caution

The seeds should not be given to pregnant women because the saponins that the seeds contain are also used in oral contraceptives and could bring on miscarriage by stimulating the uterus.

The seeds of fenugreek are dried and then used whole (above) or ground (left).

Vanilla
Vanilla planifolia

The Spanish brought vanilla to the Old World from South America, and it became one of the world's most important flavourings. It is said that Thomas Jefferson introduced it to North America upon his return from France because he missed its taste in ice cream. Now it's one of the most popular flavours.

Origins & Characteristics

The Aztecs used vanilla to flavour chocolate. Vanilla is the pod of the climbing orchid, which originated on the east coast of South America. The flowers are small and green and are fertilised by hummingbirds. When it is grown outside South America, as in Indonesia, which now produces around 80 per cent of the world's vanilla, it has to be pollinated by hand – there are no hummingbirds in Asia.

The vanilla beans (also called pods) are picked unripe and treated with steam to ferment them. The vanilla crystals, known as frost, grow on the outside of the bean, which, when dried, is long, thin and quite dark. Synthetic vanilla is now widely available, but it does not have the taste of true vanilla.

Culinary Uses

The Aztecs were right – vanilla flavours chocolate superbly. But you can also use it to flavour custards, ice creams, cakes, rice and other puddings, mousses and soufflés. Use the whole beans in preparing creams to extract the vanilla flavour from the crystals. The beans should then be removed, carefully dried and stored and reused.

Ideally, vanilla beans should be stored in sugar in an airtight container. The flavour will then leach into the sugar, which can also be used as vanilla flavoured sugar. Essence of vanilla is made by crushing the beans and soaking them in alcohol (the kind you choose depends on the flavour you require).

Medicinal Uses

Vanilla has few medicinal uses apart from aiding digestion and improving appetite.

Other Uses

A concentrated form of vanilla is used in perfumery.

Vanilla pods are picked when they are green and not yet ripe.

☕ ICED VANILLA COFFEE

You will need:
- 500ml (18fl oz) strong coffee
- 375ml (13fl oz) cold milk
- 4 tbsp sugar
- 2 vanilla beans (pods)
- 3 tbsp double cream

Mix all the ingredients together and leave in the fridge overnight. Remove the beans and serve over ice.

The vanilla plant is a climbing orchid, with waxy, fragrant flowers and fleshy leaves.

Once treated, the vanilla pods are black and sticky; split them open to scrape out the flavourful seeds.

VANILLA   105

Szechuan Pepper
Zanthoxylum piperitum

Szechuan pepper is also known as Japanese pepper, anise pepper, fagara, Chinese pepper and (rather charmingly) flower pepper, which comes from its Cantonese name *fahjiu*. A warming stimulant, Szechuan pepper can be used as a condiment in much the same way as black pepper, but it is hotter and more aromatic, and so should be used in smaller quantities. In ancient times it was used as a flavouring in foods and wines that were offered to the gods.

Origins & Characteristics

Szechuan pepper grows in the Szechuan region of China. It grows as a large tree but is now mainly cultivated as a shrub. The leaves are picked fresh and used in cooking, and the bark is stripped and dried for infusions and decoctions. The fruits are picked in summer just before they fully ripen and are dried to make the peppercorns. These can be used in a pepper mill or can be purchased already ground. It is very hot, so beware.

Culinary Uses

Chinese cuisine was often considered bland in the West until the discovery of Szechuan cooking, with its fiery pepper sauces and hot curries – all thanks to Szechuan pepper. The leaves can be used to flavour soups and savoury dishes – especially meat. They can be boiled with sugar and soy sauce and even covered in batter and fried.

Medicinal Uses

Szechuan pepper is a stimulant that works on the spleen and stomach. It also has properties that may lower blood pressure. It is diuretic and antibacterial and is used in Chinese herbal medicine as a local anaesthetic. It is very warming and, thus, good for relieving the symptoms of colds and flu.

🍲 Szechuan-Battered Prawns

You will need:
- 4 tbsp self-raising flour
- ½ tsp Szechuan pepper
- pinch of salt
- 1 piece ginger root
- 1 egg
- 5 tbsp water
- light oil for frying
- 500g (17oz) prawns

Sift flour, Szechuan pepper and salt and add finely chopped ginger. Add egg and water and beat to a batter. Heat the oil, dip each prawn in batter and deep fry for two or three minutes until golden brown. Serve hot, garnished with spring onions and a twist of lemon.

Alternatively, boil the prawns and garnish with Szechuan pepper, salt, ginger, spring onions and a twist of lemon.

When dried, the seeds of the Szechuan pepper split their casings open.

Ginger
Zingiber officinale

Undoubtedly one of the most well-known and popular spices, ginger was used widely throughout Europe in medieval times to flavour meat dishes until it fell out of favour in the eighteenth century when the spice wars pushed the price up too high. It was first mentioned in Chinese herbal medicine 2,000 years ago and remains a useful and aromatic spice for use in both culinary and medicinal roles. The young rhizomes of the plant are used for fresh ginger, while dried ginger tends to come from older, more pungent rhizomes.

Origins & Characteristics
Ginger is a perennial native to tropical Asia and is now cultivated in other tropical areas, especially Jamaica. The spice is the thick, fibrous root of *Zingiber officinale*, which grows to around 1m (3ft) tall, with long spikes of flowers that are white or yellow with purple streaks.

Culinary Uses
Fresh ginger is an important constituent of Chinese cuisine, and can be used to add flavour to many savoury dishes, especially meat. It can be used to flavour sweet dishes and is probably best known in the West as the flavouring in ginger ale.

Preserved and crystallised forms are available commercially. Stem ginger is made from the young shoots. Fresh ginger should be peeled before it is cut into thin strips or grated and added to cooking. Dried ginger is the unpeeled root that has been dried. Ground ginger can be bought commercially, but it loses its flavour quickly; it is best to buy dried and grind it or to buy it fresh if possible.

Medicinal Uses
Recent research has shown ginger to be excellent for settling the stomach, and it is now used as a travel sickness remedy. It is also a valuable source of vitamins A and B and is helpful to women suffering from morning sickness during early pregnancy.

The fresh root, if chewed, is said to alleviate sore throats as will ginger tea, which is also good for easing colic and flatulence and stimulating the appetite in invalids.

🍵 GINGER TEA

You will need:
- ½ tsp powdered root ginger
- 1 tsp honey
- 250ml (9fl oz) boiling water

Mix the powdered root with honey in the boiling water; let cool before drinking. A little dash of brandy can be added to treat colds and flu.

Ginger is a versatile spice that can be used fresh (above), dried and crumbled (left) or ground to a powder (right).

Cooking with Spices

Every country uses spices in its cooking in one form or another. And in each country, people from different regions will cook the same recipe in different ways, use different spices and quantities – and probably in every village in every region, there will be changes and additions to even the simplest of recipes. Here we will give you some ideas for basic spice recipes, but there are no rules – no exact quantities can be given that will suit all tastes and preferences. Remember, where appropriate, to bottle and refrigerate what you make as soon as possible.

Butters and Oils

An easy way to use spices in cooking is to make spicy butters and oils. Both bases take up the flavour of spices well and can then be used in recipes or as garnishes for a wide range of dishes. Spreading spiced butter on your bread will make the world of difference to your sandwiches, and a pat of spiced butter will transform the flavour of a dish of vegetables or boiled new potatoes.

SPICY BUTTERS

Spiced butters are very easy to make and are useful for spreading on fish or meat either before grilling or after, as an accompaniment. You simply cream the butter, preferably unsalted, and add your choice of spices. You can add a little black pepper and salt to taste if you think the flavour needs it. Form the butter into a roll and chill in the fridge.

Each of the following recipes is enough to flavour 250g (9oz) of butter.

Paprika Butter Use 3 tsp of paprika. Good for cooking chicken and grilled lamb.

Mustard Butter You will need 8 tsp of French or German mustard. Use with grilled meats and fish.

Juniper Butter Crush 20 juniper berries before adding to the creamed butter. Use with grilled meats.

Horseradish Butter Use 100g (4oz) of finely grated horseradish root. Use with grilled fish and meats.

Cumin Butter Use 3 tsp of ground cumin seed. Use with vegetable dishes and cheese sauces.

You might like to experiment with your own flavours from the array of spices available. Some of the other spices you could try – on their own or in a combination – include cayenne pepper, chillies, sweet peppers, coriander, mustard seed, poppy seed and sesame seed.

Start with a mild-flavoured base oil, such as a virgin olive oil, so that the spices are not overpowered.

SPICY OILS

Oils, like vinegar, will take up the flavour of spices well as long as they have sufficient time to mature. You can add spices to virgin olive oil and they will impart their flavour to your cooking as you use the oil.

Use 750ml (25fl oz) of olive oil and add six fresh chillies – green or red – 10 juniper berries, 10 sprigs of lemongrass, two sprigs of rosemary, two crushed garlic cloves and 10 black peppercorns. Store for one month to allow the flavours to develop in the oil before using.

You can make up several bottles at a time and experiment by adding other spices – you could make a milder oil by substituting sliced sweet peppers for the chillies; or use coriander, dill, caraway and fennel seeds instead of peppercorns; or you could use bay leaves instead of rosemary and lemongrass. Be sure to store your oils in the fridge.

Drinks

How cold winter would be without hot, spicy mulled wines to help us through it; somehow the heat seems to really penetrate and do us some good. But you need not limit yourself to mulled wine – there are spicy punches, mulled ales, possets, ciders, toddies, flips and wassails, too. In fact, any alcoholic drink can be served hot with added spice.

Mulled Wine Use a full-bodied red wine and add to it 3 tbsp of brown sugar, four cloves stuck into a small orange, 1 tsp allspice, 1 tsp grated nutmeg and three sticks of cinnamon. Heat gently – do not boil as this removes the alcohol – for about 10 minutes. Strain and serve with a slice of orange. Traditionally, a well-beaten egg was added to the mull just before serving. You could try heating the mixture with a red-hot poker for that genuine touch.

Lambswool Mix the flesh of four baked apples with 1l (1¾ pints) of strong dark beer (preheated), 500ml (18fl oz) of white wine, one cinnamon stick, 1 tsp of nutmeg and 1 tsp of ground ginger. Remove the cinnamon and strain. You will need to squash the mixture through the strainer. Heat again and add a little sugar to taste.

Milk Posset Heat 500ml (18fl oz) of milk and add one glass of white wine. Stir in a pinch of ground ginger and a pinch of ground nutmeg, a little sugar and a squeeze of fresh lemon juice. Serve hot.

Mulled wine has a warm and spicy aroma.

Salad Dressings

Spices can be added to a range of popular salad dressings to add that little extra bite. Spicy salad dressings make a change from the traditional French dressing and can really transform a humble salad into something special. Here are a couple of recipes to try. Both can be quickly prepared and then kept in the fridge for further use.

Spicy Chinese Salad Dressing
You will need:
• 1 garlic clove, crushed
• ½ red chilli
• 1 tbsp sesame oil
• 1 tbsp sunflower oil
• 1 tbsp cider vinegar
• 1 tsp soy sauce
• 1 tsp sherry
• 1 tsp sesame salt

Remove the membrane and seeds from the chilli and chop it finely. Mix all the ingredients together and store in a glass jar in the fridge. This salad dressing goes well with bean sprouts, stir-fried vegetables and tofu.

Spicy Cider Dressing
You will need:
• 6 tbsp cider
• juice of 1 lemon
• 2 tbsp sunflower oil
• 2 tbsp apple juice
• ½ tsp ground allspice
• ½ tsp nutmeg, grated

Mix all the ingredients together and store in a glass jar in the fridge. You may need to alter the quantities of spices to suit your taste. This dressing is sharp and gives salads a tangy lift without using too much oil.

Grated nutmeg adds a hint of sweetness to a spicy cider-based salad dressing.

Pickling Vinegars

Good cooks also need a pickling vinegar that can be used for a whole range of chutneys and relishes. There are two main types of pickling vinegar – sweet and malt. The sweet is for pickling fruit and the malt for pickling vegetables.

Sweet Pickling Vinegar

You will need:
- 1 tbsp coriander seeds
- 1 tbsp whole cloves
- 5 blades of mace
- 1 tbsp whole allspice
- 2 cinnamon sticks
- 900g (2lb) white sugar
- 1.25l (2 pints) white wine vinegar

Put the spices in a muslin bag. Mix the sugar and vinegar. Put the spice bag into the vinegar and leave to steep for six weeks in a sealed glass jar. Strain and use.

Malt Pickling Vinegar

You will need:
- 1 tsp whole cloves
- 2¼ tsp white peppercorns
- 2¼ tsp mace blades
- 1 cinnamon stick
- 2½ tsp fresh gingerroot
- 2½ tsp whole allspice
- 1.25l (2 pints) malt vinegar

Put all the spices in a muslin bag and steep in the vinegar for five to six weeks in a cool place in a tightly sealed glass jar. Shake the jar occasionally. Remove the spices and strain as required.

Bouquet Garni

No real cook would ever be without a bouquet garni – that little bag of herbs and spices used to flavour a casserole or stew for winter warmth. It's also perfect for adding a herby flavour to vinegar that will be used for pickling vegetables or in savoury chutneys. Bouquet garni are traditionally made in muslin bags, but you might like to try using the outer leaf of a leek – it will not break up during cooking.

You will need:
- 1 bay leaf
- sprig of thyme
- 1 clove
- 6 peppercorns

Place the ingredients in the bag – or leek leaf – and tie with string, leaving a good length of string hanging. Suspend the bundle inside the pot while cooking, but tie the string to the saucepan handle so that the bouquet garni does not fall into the pot and can be easily retrieved prior to serving.

You can bundle together any combination of spices and herbs you choose to make a bouquet garni to suit the flavour of any dish.

Spicy Chutneys and Relishes

Chutneys are relishes of fruit and vegetables. They make a good accompaniment to cold meats, fish, meat pies and curries. They can range from relatively mild to very hot. The word 'chutney' comes from the Hindu word *chatni*, which means 'strong sweet relish' – and that's exactly what it is.

Sweet Pepper Chutney

You will need:

- 3kg (6½lb) large ripe tomatoes
- 500g (1lb) onions
- 3 garlic cloves, crushed
- 3 red sweet peppers
- 3 green sweet peppers
- 1 tsp ground mace
- 1 tsp ground black pepper
- 1 tsp paprika
- grated rind and juice of 2 lemons
- grated rind and juice of 1 orange
- 1 tsp ground ginger
- pinch of cayenne pepper
- 50g (2oz) salt
- 450ml (16fl oz) white wine vinegar
- 250g (9oz) brown sugar

Seed tomatoes after scalding and peeling them – you only want the flesh, not the seeds. Chop the onions and garlic and add to the tomato flesh in a saucepan. Prepare peppers by removing the seeds and membranes. Slice and add to the pan. Add all the other ingredients and heat gently until all the sugar has dissolved. Stir. Bring to a boil and simmer for two hours, stirring occasionally. When the chutney is thick and rich, you can store it in glass jars. Store in a cool place for two months before using – this is a mild chutney that will go well with cold meats and fish.

Spices give a kick to chutneys and relishes that go particularly well with cheeses and cold meats.

Spicy Lemon and Lime Relish

You will need:

- 500ml (18fl oz) olive oil
- 5 lemons
- 5 limes
- 2 tbsp black peppercorns
- 1 chopped dried red chilli
- 1 tbsp cumin seeds
- 3 tbsp salt
- 4 garlic cloves, crushed
- 1 tbsp white mustard seeds
- 3 bay leaves
- 1 small piece of fresh ginger, grated

In a saucepan, heat the oil thoroughly and let it cool. Slice the lemons and limes into quarters. Grind the peppercorns, chilli and cumin seeds together and sprinkle over the lemons and limes. Add the rest of the ingredients and stir thoroughly. Let the mixture settle for one hour and then pour into a glass jar. Pour over the cooled oil and leave, sealed, in a warm place for one week, shaking every day. Then store in a dark cupboard for one month. The rinds will then have softened and taken on the spices and oil. Serve with hot curries and plain rice. This relish should keep for up to six months – if you have not eaten it all by then – and goes extremely well with curries.

Try this spicy relish with a curry instead of the traditional hot lime pickle.

Curries

Most people think of India and China when they hear of curries, and although they do make up a large part of both Indian and Chinese cuisine, there are many other countries that have curry recipes as well, such as Mexico, Thailand and the Caribbean nations.

Match your spices to the curry, so use cardamom, cinnamon, cloves and ginger if you want a fresh sweet flavour; turmeric and fenugreek for a slightly more robust sour taste; and cumin and coriander seeds for a fuller, more solid flavour. Only use 1 to 2 tbsp of ground spice blends in a curry for four people – this keeps the taste distinctive and delicate but not overpowering. Fry the spices when you begin cooking because this will develop their flavours, but be careful not to burn them because they will be bitter if you do. For Malaysian curries you should add lemongrass for that distinctive flavour. Thai curries are always part of a selection of dishes in a main meal, and the hotness is usually offset by a sweeter or blander dish;

they often include lemongrass, galangal and kaffir lime leaves.

Curry powder and garam masala (page 128), are both dry spice blends you can store for up to four months. If you plan to grind your own spices so that you are always using them fresh, it's a good idea to keep a separate coffee grinder specifically for this purpose so that your coffee doesn't taste too spicy afterwards.

You might also like to make your own curry paste. You can use this immediately to cook any of the tikka curry dishes – hot curries using yogurt that were traditionally cooked in a *tandoor* (clay oven).

Garam masala is a blend of dried, ground spices, including cinnamon, cumin and cloves.

Curry Paste

You will need:

- 1½ tsp cumin seeds
- 1 tsp garam masala
- 1 tsp garlic powder
- ½ tsp paprika
- 1 tsp turmeric
- pinch of salt
- 2 tbsp wine vinegar
- 1½ tsp coriander seeds
- 1½ tsp chilli powder
- 1 tsp dried mint
- 1 tbsp water
- 2 tbsp olive oil
- dash of lemon juice

Grind the seeds in a coffee grinder and add to the other dry ingredients. Stir well, add the water, lemon juice and vinegar and mix into a thin paste. Heat the oil slowly in a heavy frying pan and stir in the paste. Cook gently until all the water has been absorbed (this will take about 10 minutes). You can then use this paste as is, or you can store it in an airtight glass jar – you might like to pour a tiny amount of oil on top of the mixture to keep it really fresh. Once you have this paste it can be used to make a tikka masala – *masala* means 'hot', by the way, so you have been warned.

Ginger, nutmeg, coriander seeds, cinnamon, turmeric and more: a curry paste has great depth of flavour from a multitude of ingredients.

Chicken Tikka Masala

You will need:

- 4 chicken breasts
- 4 tbsp plain yogurt
- 6 tbsp curry paste
- 2 tbsp olive oil
- 1 clove garlic, crushed
- 1 onion, chopped
- small piece of fresh ginger, grated
- 1 red chilli, chopped
- 1 tbsp almonds, ground
- 1 tbsp tomato purée
- 250ml (9fl oz) water
- 45g (1½oz) butter, melted
- 125ml (4fl oz) double cream
- dash of lemon juice

To serve:

- 1 tsp cumin seeds
- 4 sprigs of fresh coriander
- 300ml (10fl oz) plain yogurt

Skin and cube the chicken and put in a bowl with the yogurt and half the tikka paste. Stir well and marinate for half an hour. Heat the oil in a heavy pan and fry the garlic, onion, ginger and chilli for four minutes, then add the remaining tikka paste and fry for three minutes. Add the almonds, tomato purée and water and simmer for 15 minutes.

Brush the chicken with the melted butter and grill for 15 minutes, turning until the meat is cooked through. You can now put the tikka mixture through a blender if you want a smoother masala. Add the cream and lemon juice to the tikka sauce and then the chicken. Simmer for five minutes.

This should be served hot with naan bread and a garnish of toasted cumin seeds, fresh coriander and plain yogurt. A spicy rice (page 124) makes a good accompaniment.

Spicy Rice

You will need:

- 2 onions, finely chopped
- 125ml (4fl oz) vegetable oil
- 1 tsp turmeric
- ½ tsp cumin
- ½ tsp coriander seeds
- ½ tsp cardamom
- ¼ tsp cloves, finely ground
- 250g (9oz) rice
- pinch of salt
- 500ml (18fl oz) hot water

Brown the onions in the hot oil in a heavy pan, add the spices and fry for two minutes.

Add the rice, washed and drained, and the salt, and brown for two minutes, then pour in the water so that it just covers the rice by about 2.5cm (1in).

Cover the pan and simmer for 15 minutes – or until all the water has been absorbed. Fluff with a fork and serve hot.

This is a basic recipe, and you can add any other spices that you want – a little cayenne pepper will give the rice a bite, or you could swap the turmeric for paprika if you want your rice red rather than yellow. For a plain rice you can leave out the spices and just colour it with turmeric or paprika.

In India, rice is usually fried before boiling, while in China the rice is usually boiled then fried with the meat and vegetables. To make a pilau rice you can add almonds and raisins – lightly sauté them before adding them to the cooked rice.

Use your favourite flavours in spicy rice; cloves, cumin seed and cardamom are a good basic combination.

Sweet and Spicy Treats

After you've eaten all that spicy food, what could be better than something a little spicy-sweet to cleanse the palate and sweeten the breath? Spices are not only good for savoury dishes but also for sweets, puddings and desserts. You may like to try the following recipes.

Cardamom Ice Cream

You will need:

• 16 whole green cardamom pods
• 250ml (9fl oz) whole milk
• 350ml (12fl oz) double cream
• 4 egg yolks
• 75g (3oz) icing sugar

Bruise 10 of the cardamom pods and heat with the milk and half the cream to almost boiling point for two minutes. Let the mixture cool for 10 minutes.

Remove the seeds from the remaining cardamom pods and crush them in a pestle and mortar or with the end of a rolling pin in a bowl.

Whisk the egg yolks with the sugar. Strain the milk mixture to remove the cardamom pods and add the liquid

to the eggs and sugar. Whisk thoroughly and heat until it begins to thicken. Remove from the heat and allow to cool again.

Whip the other half of the cream and add the crushed cardamom seeds. Fold into the cooled milk and egg mixture. Freeze for two hours. Remove from the freezer and whisk to break up the ice crystals, then return to the freezer overnight or for at least 12 hours.

The combination of sweet and spice when you add cardamom to a dish is unexpected and delicious.

Spicy Winter Compote

You will need:

- 175g (6oz) each of dried peaches, pears, apricots and raisins
- 125g (5oz) icing sugar
- 600ml (1 pint) water
- 175ml (6fl oz) red wine
- 6 allspice berries
- 2 cinnamon sticks
- 6 cloves
- 1 vanilla bean
- 8 peppercorns
- 175ml (6fl oz) port

Soak the dried fruit in hot water for 10 minutes. Add the fresh pears, peeled, cored and quartered. Add the sugar and cook over a low heat for five minutes. Add everything else except the port and simmer gently for four minutes. Remove from the heat, add the port and let steep for 10 minutes. Serve warm – it is very good with cardamom ice cream (page 125).

Cardamom Honey Dressing

You will need:

- 300ml (½ pint) clear honey
- 2 tbsp lemon juice
- a few drops of orange-flower water
- ½ tsp cracked cardamom seed

Beat the honey in a mixer until it is light in colour. Gradually add the lemon juice and orange flower water, then stir in the cardamom seed.

This is a delicious dressing for fruit salads. Keep it in an airtight jar in the fridge.

This winter compote is served both hot and spicy.

Spice Combinations

By tradition, there are various spice blends that have become known and loved throughout the world. India has produced many spice mixtures for its vast cuisine, possibly the most well known being garam masala, while Europe's famous combination is quatre-épices and there are established spice mixtures that are used for specific purposes, such as pickling and pudding spice. The following pages give recipes for some popular combinations, but don't be afraid to experiment with your own.

Despite being known and used the world over, the recipes for some of these popular combinations are the subject of fierce debate and argument. For example, where we might suggest that garam masala is made with only 4 tsp of black cumin seeds, some authorities would argue vociferously that you simply cannot make a good garam masala without using at least 5 tsp. Or we might suggest that a good curry powder would have, among its other ingredients, 1 tsp of black pepper to 2 tsp of cinnamon, but others will disagree and say that you absolutely, and without exception, must use exactly 2¼ tsp. Combining spices is that sort of area – it allows everyone to find their own particular favourite and become an instant expert. We hope you too will follow this path and become a spice combination connoisseur.

Try to buy seeds and spices that are as fresh as possible. Heat the seeds in the oven for a few minutes or in a heavy frying pan until you can detect the strong aroma. Then you should grind the seeds – a pestle and mortar is the traditional tool to use, but a coffee grinder works well, too, and can give a faster and more evenly ground result. You may find that your coffee tastes a little strange for a while unless you can set aside a grinder dedicated specifically for grinding spices.

Once ground, the seeds should be put through a coarse strainer to remove any stalks, husks or other inedible foreign matter, such as small stones.

A pestle and mortar is the traditional tool for grinding spices.

Keep the ground spices in individual, airtight glass jars – clearly labelled, as many will look very similar to one another – in a cool dark place. If you can use dark glass jars, that will be even better. Only mix combinations together in quantities that you can use in a week or two at the most; spice combinations will lose their potency quite quickly after that.

All the following recipes are ones we have tried and like – you may, however, wish to experiment and find your own favourite combinations.

All the measurements are given in teaspoons and these quantities refer to flat teaspoonfuls, not rounded or heaped.

Hot Curry Powder
• 2 tsp chilli powder
• 1 tsp cloves
• 2 tsp cardamom pods
• 2 tsp ground cinnamon
• 2½ tsp ground cumin
• ½ tsp ground fenugreek
• 1 tsp ground nutmeg
• 2 tsp ground black pepper
• 1 tsp mustard seed
• 1 tsp black poppy seed
• 1 tsp curry leaf

Mild Curry Powder
• 1 tsp chilli powder
• 1 tsp ground black pepper
• 1 tsp ground cumin
• 4 tsp coriander seeds
• 1½ tsp ground turmeric
• 1 tsp cardamom pods
• 1 tsp ground fenugreek

Garam masala is often mistaken for curry powder, but it is not the same. It might be as hot and as spicy, but it has a different flavour altogether. You can make a dry masala or a wet paste masala. Here are recipes for both.

Dry Garam Masala
• 3 tsp ground black pepper
• 2 tsp ground cinnamon
• 2½ tsp ground cumin
• 2½ tsp cloves
• 1½ tsp ground mace
• 1½ tsp cardamom pods
• 2 tsp bay leaves

Wet Paste Garam Masala
• 6 tsp coriander seeds
• 3 tsp ground black cumin
• 3 tsp cardamom pods
• 1 tsp bay leaves
• 4 tsp ground black pepper
• 1 tsp ground nutmeg
• 3 tsp ground cinnamon
• juice of 2 lemons or limes
Mix all the ingredients together to make a paste.

Chinese five-spice powder is a mixture of ground cloves, cassia, star anise, aniseed and fennel seed (clockwise from above).

Chinese Five-Spice

Chinese five-spice is used extensively in Chinese cuisine. We have suggested equal quantities for the blend as a starting point – you can then experiment as you will. Be warned, though, that this combination is quite hot.

- 1 tsp fennel seed
- 1 tsp aniseed
- 1 tsp star anise
- 1 tsp ground cassia
- 1 tsp cloves

There is a Japanese equivalent to Chinese five-spice, known as seven-flavour spice, which includes pepper leaf, sesame seed, poppy seed, hemp seed, rapeseed and dried tangerine peel. It may be best if you buy this one commercially prepared because getting some of the ingredients may be difficult – if not illegal – in some countries.

French Quatre-Épices (Four-Spice)

This recipe is a traditional French spice mixture that is used to flavour cold meats and as a general spice blend for seasoning – it is quite hot.

- 6 tsp ground white pepper
- 1 tsp whole cloves
- 1 tsp ground ginger
- 1 tsp ground nutmeg

OTHER COMBINATIONS

You might like to try your hand at *aliño criolo*, which is a Venezuelan combination of annatto seed, fresh oregano, ground cumin, paprika, garlic salt and black pepper. Fresh garlic is added just before using this in cooking stews and casseroles.

Or how about *sambal*, which is a spicy relish much loved in India and China? You need fresh chillies, a little sugar, salt, oil, some lemon juice, onion, lemongrass and dried shrimp. They are all blended together to make a hot, spicy pickle-like relish to accompany any Indian or Chinese dish.

Others include: Cajun mix, used with Mexican fried beans, which consists of paprika, chilli, cumin, mustard and oregano; pumpkin pie mix, which consists of cinnamon, allspice, nutmeg and ginger; and *zahtar*, used to flavour meatballs and hamburgers – a blend of sumac, roasted sesame seeds and thyme.

Sweet Peppers

Some people have never tried sweet peppers (*Capsicum annuum*) because they think they are just fat versions of chillies. Nothing could be further from the truth. Sweet peppers are juicy and tasty without any of the fire that chillies have.

Although all chillies are capsicums, not all capsicums are chillies. Sweet peppers (page 30) are mild and sweet. They can be sliced and eaten raw, added to salads, stir-fried, added to casseroles and stews, or stuffed. They can be grilled on their own as vegetables. They are also known as 'bell fruit'.

Technically, the green sweet peppers are unripe fruit, but they taste very similar to the red and yellow varieties, although they may be a little more bitter. You can blanch them for a minute or two before cooking to remove the bitter flavour. You can also get cream-coloured peppers. Before cooking them, you should slit them open and remove the seeds and membrane. These can be quite hot and bitter. If you buy sweet peppers in jars or tins, the seeds should have been removed already, although there should

be no need to buy them as such anymore – fresh sweet peppers are now available all year round in most countries.

When buying sweet peppers always look for smooth, firm skins and a good colour. There shouldn't be any softness or discolouration. If they have gone soft in any places, they have already started to go bad and should not be bought. Peppers will keep in the fridge for three or four days or in a cool pantry for two or three days.

To freeze them, remove the seeds and membranes and slice them lengthwise. Blanch them for two minutes. Cool them under cold running water for two minutes and then drain and freeze them. You can keep them for 12 months in a freezer. When you want to use them, you can add the frozen slices directly to any recipe. If you prefer pepper halves, blanch them for three minutes and defrost for an hour before using.

Sweet peppers are the main ingredient in ratatouille (a French vegetable stew). They make a good accompaniment to grilled meat or baked potatoes.

Slice peppers lengthwise rather than across their flesh. The juice and flavour will stay in better.

Ratatouille

You will need:
- 2 aubergines
- salt
- 5 tomatoes
- 1 large green sweet pepper
- 1 large red or orange sweet pepper
- 6 medium courgettes
- 3 tbsp olive oil
- 2 medium onions
- 2 garlic cloves
- ½ tsp coriander seeds
- salt and pepper to taste

Slice the aubergines, sprinkle them with a little salt and let them drain. This will help to remove some of their bitterness. Skin and chop the tomatoes, crush the garlic cloves, and slice open the peppers and remove the seeds and membranes. Slice the courgettes. Peel and coarsely chop the onions.

Heat the oil and gently cook the onions, garlic and peppers for about 10 minutes. Add the aubergine and the remainder of the ingredients. Cover and simmer for about 45 minutes, stirring occasionally to prevent the ratatouille from sticking.

You can try experimenting by adding a little Tabasco sauce if you like your ratatouille a little hotter. Garnish your ratatouille with finely chopped parsley if you want to add some colour.

Grilled Sweet Peppers

You will need:
• selection of sweet peppers

You can use any colour of peppers, but remember that the green ones may be a little more bitter than the red or yellow.

Slice your peppers into two halves and remove the seeds and membranes. Lightly toast on the grill on both sides until the flesh just begins to bubble and brown. You can serve grilled sweet peppers just as they are – hot and succulent – or cut them into smaller pieces to add them to kebabs. They slide onto skewers well and should be cooked until the flesh bubbles.

Basque Piperade

You will need:
• 1 large red pepper
• 1 large green pepper
• 6 tomatoes
• 2 onions
• 1 garlic clove
• 50g (2oz) butter
• 6 eggs
• 3 tbsp milk
• 10 slices of bacon

This is a recipe from the Basque region of Spain. Prepare the vegetables and garlic in the same way as for ratatouille and cook them all in the butter for eight minutes. Beat the eggs and milk as you would for an omelette. Pour over the vegetables and reduce the heat to a simmer. Fry the bacon separately. When the eggs are just set but still creamy on the top, lay the cooked bacon over them and serve hot.

Once grilled and cool enough to handle, the charred skin of the peppers can be peeled from the flesh, if you prefer.

Chillies come in a wide range of colours, shapes and sizes, as well as a sliding scale of fieriness.

Chillies

No one really knows who grew the first chillies – but we do know it was around 9,000 years ago in the Amazon region of South America. Today there are more than 150 varieties of chillies, and they are grown worldwide, but principally in Mexico, California, Texas, New Mexico, Arizona, Thailand, India, Africa and Asia.

It was the original inhabitants of Mexico who first used chillies in their cooking. Once the Spanish and Portuguese explorers tasted them, their use spread to Europe and beyond. It was not too long before they had made it as far as China. Today chillies are known for their fiery pungency and for enhancing Mexican and Asian cuisine.

Chillies (page 32) are members of the *capsicum* family (Latin for 'box' – a box of seeds) and are the fruit of the *Capsicum frutescens* plant, which will grow in any warm, humid climate. They are easy to grow at home in pots, and make interesting and useful houseplants. They will cross-pollinate easily, so keep them separate if you want to stick to a particular variety.

By tradition, the smaller chillies have always been regarded as the hottest, but that may not necessarily be true. Chillies range from mildly hot to the extremely hot, and great care must be exercised when handling them. Ideally you should wear thin surgical rubber gloves and wash your hands afterwards.

Never rub your eyes or face when handling chillies in any form – the oil they contain is an irritant and will burn. If you do get any on your skin, wash it off with copious amounts of cold milk or soap and water.

If you get any in your eyes, flush with lots of cool water. If you eat chillies and find them too hot, drink cold milk to reduce the fieriness – it's far more effective than gulping down water. Keep chillies away from children.

Chillies come in all shapes, sizes and colours – from long thin ones to short plump ones; from red to green, purple, orange, yellow, cream and black. They can be bought fresh, dried, pickled in brine or powdered. Dried chillies can be hotter than fresh ones. Whichever variety you choose, if the seeds are used, the chillies will be hotter and more bitter than if you only use the flesh.

CHILLI VARIETIES

Chillies each have a unique flavour and heat level. On these pages you will find some, but by no means all, of the most popular chillies – each has been graded from one to five for hotness – with five being the hottest.

FRESH CHILLIES

Anaheim This is also known as the Californian chilli or the New Mexican chilli. The fruit is about 15cm (6in) long and either bright green or, fully ripened, red. When it is dried and powdered, the Anaheim chilli is sold as 'Colorado chilli powder'. Quite mild in flavour – about a one on the hotness scale.

Jalapeno

Jalapeno This is one of the most commonly used chillies and is grown in Mexico and across the North American southwest. Dried and smoked, it is known as a chipotle. When fresh, it is a juicy, plump chilli 6–8cm (2–3in) long and can be red or, when unripe, green. The red ones are most flavoursome. A middling heat – a two or three.

Malaguetta This is a very hot (and tiny) chilli from Brazil. Its heat rating is about a five. It is thin and comes in green (unripe) and red (ripe).

Poblano This one is quite mild – about a two. It is green or red, 10–15cm (4–6in) long with quite thick flesh. When it is dried, it is known as an ancho. It comes from Mexico and California.

Serrano This is a very thin chilli, red or green in colour and 5cm (2in) long with a clean, sweet taste. It is fairly hot – about a four – but flavourful as well. The red ones are definitely sweeter than the green.

Bird's eye

Bird's Eye This is a tiny chilli, but what it lacks in size it makes up for in strength! Very hot – five.

Anaheim

Habanero This is a distinct five, and more. It comes in any colour from red to green to purple and is about 5cm (2in) long. When it is ripe and red, it is said to have a fruity, tropical flavour, but the heat may not let you taste much. This is probably one of the hottest chillies available. It is grown in Central America and the Caribbean.

Scotch Bonnet Here is another of the very hot ones (five +), and it is grown in Jamaica and the Caribbean. It is only 2.5cm (1in) long, but it packs a punch. It is usually described as having a smoky, fruity flavour, but the heat may stop you from tasting anything.

Scotch bonnet

DRIED CHILLIES

Chillies are dried because they last longer this way and are easier to transport. Here is a selection.

Ancho This is the dried poblano chilli. It has a sweet, fruity flavour and is quite mild – about a two. It is usually reddish brown with wrinkled skin.

Cayenne This one is grown and dried in Louisiana and Mexico and is quite hot – about four or five. It is used to make the famous cayenne pepper. It is the quintessential chilli: about 5–10cm (2–4in) long, bright red and tapering to a point.

Mulato

Cayenne

Mulato This is another popular mild dried chilli, also from central Mexico, 10–14cm (4–5½in) long with a dark brown skin. It has a smoky flavour reminiscent of licorice and rates a one or two for heat.

New Mexican These come in many colours – from pale olive to bright scarlet. They are quite mild, a one or two, with a full chilli flavour not masked by excessive fieriness.

Pasilla This is a moderately mild chilli, about a three, from central Mexico. It is about 15cm (6in) long with an almost black skin, shiny and wrinkled. Some pasillas can be very hot, so choose carefully. You can also get powdered pasilla.

Guajillo A mild dried chilli from central Mexico, it is widely available, 10–15cm (4–6in) long with a rough, burgundy-coloured skin and a slight bitter flavour. The skin is a bit tough and should be removed before using.

USING CHILLIES

Most people will have heard of chilli con carne, but there are many other uses for chillies – where would India be without chillies for its curries? The Szechuan region of China produces some very hot chillies for use in Chinese cooking, but it is probably Mexican and Caribbean cuisine that most people associate with chillies – and rightly so. No true Mexican would go very long without eating *mole poblano*, which is the traditional dish of Mexico – and how about guacamole made with chillies and avocados?

In tropical regions, chillies, with their fiery taste, are used to flavour bland tasting staple foods, and in India they are used in rice, as well as being a staple ingredient in many curry powders. Chillies are now even used to flavour vodka.

As stated before, always remember to exercise caution when using chillies, hold them well away from your face when cutting them and don't rub your eyes. If possible, wear a pair of household rubber gloves. Fresh chillies help in digesting starches and are rich in vitamin C. But always remember – a little goes a long way.

Mole Poblano

You will need:
- 4 large chicken pieces
- 1 onion, chopped
- 1 tbsp olive oil
- 1 each of pasilla, ancho and mulato chillies (or any 3 dried chillies if you cannot get these), chopped
- 2 cloves garlic, crushed
- 6 tomatoes, chopped
- 2 tbsp sesame seeds
- 2 tbsp whole almonds
- 2 tbsp peanuts
- ½ tsp coriander seeds
- 1 square dark chocolate

Cook the chicken with the onions and olive oil in a large, heavy pan until the chicken is browned. Remove the chicken and dry. Add the chillies, garlic and tomatoes to the oil and cooked onions and cook thoroughly for about 10 minutes.

Grind all the nuts and seeds in a pestle and mortar or a coffee grinder, add to the cooking chillies and cook for an additional five minutes. Take a little of the cooked juices, dissolve the square of chocolate in it and pour this back into the pan. Put the chicken back into the pan, too and bring to a boil. Then simmer until the chicken is cooked through.

You can add a little water if the sauce is getting too thick. Serve hot, with a fresh salad.

PREPARING CHILLIES

Fresh chillies should be sliced in half, and their seeds should be removed. You can then lightly grill them, and the skin will peel off easily. They are then ready to use. Some people like to grill them before removing the seeds because there is less risk of the volatile oil getting on their skin.

To remove the skin of a chilli, drop the chilli into a plastic bag and peel it safely in that. Washing the peeled chillies will remove the oil – and much of the pungency.

Dried chillies should be lightly roasted and then soaked in hot water for about 10 minutes to rehydrate them. You may need to remove their seeds.

Remember that the heat of the chillies is in the membrane rather than the seeds, so make sure you remove all of the membrane before use – chillies are hot enough without adding to their fieriness.

When buying fresh chillies, look for firm, shiny specimens with good colour. They should be dry and heavy. Any that are

limp, dull or discoloured should be rejected. When you get them home, rinse and dry them, and store them in the salad drawer of your fridge. They should keep for two or three weeks. If you do not keep them in the fridge, they will deteriorate fairly quickly. They will also spoil if you keep them in a plastic bag because of the moisture build-up.

Chillies are hot, but they also have a flavour. Experienced chilli eaters will often claim they can identify quite delicate flavours and tastes in chillies that people less used to them will not be able to discern. When you first start eating chillies, you will find they all just taste hot, but within

a short period of time you will become more tolerant of their heat and be able to eat hotter varieties and experience their actual flavours. What one person describes as mild or hot may be completely different for another – only you can decide your own preferences. Do not be bullied into eating chillies that are hotter than you really like.

Always remove the seeds from inside a chilli before use. They are very hot and bitter to taste.

Mustard

Mustard is incredibly easy to grow and thrives in temperate climates, so it is, unsurprisingly, one of the most common and widely used of all spices. The Romans were probably first to recognise its importance in cooking, and they spread it to all the parts of their empire.

There are two basic types of mustard – brown (page 26) and white (page 98). The brown mustard seeds are more aromatic and tasty, while the white ones are larger and hotter. Mustards the world over are combinations of these two types of seeds.

English Mustard Made from a combination of both white and brown seeds (roughly 20 per cent white and 80 per cent brown) mixed with flour and turmeric. It is often sold as a dry, bright yellow powder. Cold water is added to this to make a traditional hot English mustard. It should always be allowed to stand for 10 minutes to let the flavour develop.

French Mustards There are two types: Dijon and Bordeaux.

Dijon Mustard Made from brown seeds that are husked and ground and mixed with verjuice (unripe grape juice). It is used to flavour mayonnaise and sauces.

Bordeaux Mustard Made with whole seeds and mixed with vinegar, sugar and tarragon. It is used as an accompaniment to cold meats.

German Mustards Very similar to Bordeaux mustards, but they are usually flavoured with spices, herbs and caramel, which tend to make them darker and tastier. They are good eaten with cold meats and sausages.

American Mustard Made from powdered white seeds and flour, vinegar and colouring. It is excellent with hot dogs and hamburgers.

English mustard (top) is hotter than Dijon (below).

MUSTARD COMBINATIONS

English Whole-Grain This is a pungent, hot mustard made from whole white seeds with white wine, black pepper and allspice.

Green Peppercorn Mustard It is made with Dijon mustard with crushed green peppercorns added to it and is popular in Burgundy, where it is eaten with grilled meat. It is quite hot and spicy.

White Wine Mustard This is another Dijon mustard made with white wine. Quite hot, it is used for flavouring sauces.

Tarragon Mustard This Bordeaux-type mustard is flavoured with tarragon. It is quite mild and is excellent with other spicy foods.

Düsseldorf Mustard As its name implies, it is very popular in Düsseldorf. Although a type of German mustard, it is without the spices and caramel, but it is not nearly as mild as German mustard and is best eaten with spicy food.

Moutarde de Meaux This is a Dijon mustard made with whole brown seeds – nicely hot and best eaten with foods that are not so spicy.

Coarse Grain Mustard This is a type of *Moutarde de Meaux* which has white wine added to it. It is quite hot.

Florida Mustard This is a Bordeaux mustard made with wine from the Champagne region rather than vinegar.

Once you have tried all of the commercially available mustards, you can start experimenting with your own. Try mixing white and brown seeds, husked or whole, adding herbs and spices, using vinegar or wine – even adding a little honey, caramel or garlic.

Mustard can be used in a vast variety of ways in cooking, adding extra zest to pickles, relishes and salad dressings. It makes a wonderful addition to all cheese dishes, really bringing out the flavour of the cheese. Cheese on toast will never taste the same again! And mustard mayonnaise spices up ordinary salad dishes.

Mustard Mayonnaise

You will need:
- 1 egg yolk
- ½ tbsp mustard of your choice
- ½ tsp Worcestershire sauce
- 1 tsp white wine
- salt and pepper to taste
- 3 drops Tabasco sauce
- 250ml (9fl oz) fine cooking oil such as sunflower or olive oil
- juice of half a lemon

Blend together everything except the lemon juice in a little of the oil. Add the rest of the oil, blending slowly. Then add the lemon juice while still blending.

Spice Vinegars

It is hard to believe that the vinegar we use to make vinaigrette dressing and to pickle and preserve spices and herbs is actually an acid – and so corrosive that you should only use stainless steel, earthenware, glass or enamelled pots when using it in cooking.

Vinegar is made from the fermentation of wine, cider or malted barley, which is then flavoured with herbs or spices.

Wine Vinegar The best wine vinegar is made by slowly fermenting wine until it turns acetic. It should then stand for a month before use. You can get red and white wine vinegar. Most people use white wine vinegar in vinaigrette dressing and mayonnaise because red wine vinegar will turn everything pink. Red wine vinegar is, however, the more flavourful of the two.

Malt Vinegar Malt vinegar is made from malted barley and is brown in colour. This colour is added by mixing the vinegar with caramel. Malt vinegar used to be judged by its colour – the darker the brown, the stronger the vinegar, but nowadays it is often coloured artificially. Malt vinegar is best used for pickling.

Cider Vinegar Cider vinegar is, as its name suggests, made from fermented cider. It has a distinctive taste and is halfway between wine vinegar and malt vinegar in its strength of flavour. Cider vinegar is best used for chutneys and fruity relishes.

To make the following spice vinegars, you can use any of the vinegars mentioned here as a base, but a good white wine vinegar is best. A distilled vinegar will give you a purer flavour of the spices. These vinegars can be used to make mayonnaise and vinaigrette sauces or poured over salads. They can also be used as pickling vinegars.

Basic Spice Vinegar
You will need:
• spice seeds – approximately 2–3 tbsp spice to 1l (1¾ pints) vinegar

Lightly bruise any spice seeds in a mortar. Put the crushed seeds into the vinegar and shake well. Put the spice vinegar in a warm, dark place for two weeks and give it an occasional shake. At the end of this time, taste the vinegar. If you want a stronger tasting spice vinegar, strain off the mixture and discard the seeds. Flavour the vinegar with a fresh batch of spices and ferment again. Taste again at the end of two weeks. You can do this as many times as you want until you reach the required strength, but once will be enough with most spice vinegars. When you have the desired strength, strain off the seeds and store your new vinegar in a corked bottle.

TYPES OF SPICE VINEGARS

All these recipes give quantities for 750ml (26fl oz) of vinegar. You can use white or brown or try a combination of both.

Mustard Vinegar Add 3 tbsp of crushed mustard seeds.

Chilli Vinegar Use six hot, red chillies and one whole garlic clove. Leave for two weeks then strain thoroughly. Experiment with different types of chilli.

Coriander Vinegar Use 3 tbsp crushed coriander seeds.

Ginger Vinegar Use one whole root peeled and finely chopped.

Spicy Vinegar Use 1 tbsp of crushed black peppercorns, 1 tsp of crushed celery seed, 1 tsp of peeled and chopped fresh gingerroot, one dried chilli, one cinnamon stick, 1 tsp of allspice. Simmer all of the spices together in the vinegar. Let cool and store for two weeks. Strain and bottle.

Very Spicy Vinegar Put two garlic cloves, six hot red chillies, 2 tsp of black peppercorns, 2 tsp of juniper berries, four sprigs of lemongrass and four sprigs of rosemary into the vinegar and store for two weeks.

Quick Chilli Vinegar Add 2 tsp of hot chilli sauce to the vinegar and use immediately.

Spiced vinegars add interest to salad dressings and heat to homemade pickles.

Worcestershire Sauce Although not strictly a vinegar, this can be used in the same way. You need six garlic cloves, 1 tsp of black pepper, ¼ tsp of chilli powder, 350ml (12fl oz) of vinegar, 5 tbsp of soy sauce. Blend all the ingredients together in a blender. This is now ready to use, but store it in an airtight bottle and shake well before use each time.

Spices for Beauty & Health

It may be easier to buy synthetically produced perfumes, face creams, incense and massage oils, but it is not as satisfying as producing your own special and unique blends. Spices are evocative and pungent – they bring the enigmatic Orient, or the sun of the Caribbean, or a hint of the mysterious lost civilisations of South America into our homes.

Spices for Relaxation

The smell of spices is an evocative aroma, often associated with winter or – more specifically – Christmas. In the past, the pungent aroma of spices was often used to hide the smells of unwashed bodies and to purify and cleanse the air. Many traditions burn incense as part of their religious rites, but at home it is also an excellent way to create a calm and soothing environment in which you can truly relax.

INCENSE

Many of us have at one time or another used incense to add a spicy aroma to our homes just because it smells good. We also know that in China, since the earliest times, incense has been used as a magic potion – a charm against restless ghosts. Whether you want some incense to settle your own ghosts, to add ritual and mystery to your home or merely to add aroma, the following recipes produce incense that will soothe and relax you – and from a relaxed person comes inner beauty.

Traditionally there have been two ways to burn incense – loose and sprinkled onto glowing charcoal, or blended with charcoal and gum and shaped into sticks or cones. The gummed incense needs a good draft to burn, which is why in churches the incense burner is swung backwards and forwards to help the charcoal to glow.

Remember that when burning incense, the fumes may be toxic, so always make sure you have adequate ventilation.

Ground cassia bark is a good base ingredient for incense.

Loose Incense

You will need:

- 25g (1oz) gum benzoin (from a pharmacist)
- 25g (1oz) powdered sandalwood
- 20g (¾oz) ground cassia bark
- 20g (¾oz) ground cardamom seeds
- 15g (½oz) ground cloves

Mix together all the ingredients; the gum acts as a fixative. This is a basic incense recipe, so experiment with your own favourite combinations.

Shaped Incense

You will need:

- 10g (¼oz) powdered sandalwood
- 10g (¼oz) ground cassia bark
- 100g (3½oz) gum arabic
- 25g (1oz) powdered gum benzoin
- 200g (7oz) charcoal

Crush the charcoal and add it to the dry ingredients. Make a stiff paste with the gum arabic and some water, then stir in the rest of the ingredients. Form the incense into any shape you want and let dry for a day or two. Use this basic recipe and add any other ingredients you like.

PERFUME

Slice five vanilla beans and immerse in pure alcohol. Leave for six weeks but shake daily. At the end of this, strain the alcohol off, and you will have a pleasantly refreshing perfume.

POT POURRI

A spicy pot pourri will add a heavy, pungent scent to any room and give you an invigorating aroma. To make a dry pot pourri, you can blend and grind any spices that you want – you can experiment and add spices as you try them in your cooking.

A basic pot pourri mixture would use rose petals as a base, or you could try crushed bay leaves. Then add to this base finely ground allspice, cassia, cinnamon, aniseed, nutmeg, vanilla bean, coriander seeds, cloves, ginger, cardamom and mace. Here are two other spicy pot pourri combinations you might like to try.

A light, refreshing, springtime pot pourri mixture
You will need:
- 50g (2oz) caraway
- 50g (2oz) cardamom
- 50g (2oz) cinnamon
- 50g (2oz) fennel
- 2 marigold flowers
- 6 drops neroli essential oil
- 6 drops lemongrass essential oil

A rich pot pourri mixture with an aroma of Christmas
You will need:
- 25g (1oz) cinnamon sticks
- 50g (2oz) cloves
- 50g (2oz) star anise
- 50g (2oz) juniper berries
- 50g (2oz) black pepper
- 50g (2oz) myrtle leaves
- 25g (1oz) rosemary
- 6 drops essential oil of frankincense
- 2 drops essential oil of cinnamon
- 6 drops essential oil of orange
- 2 drops essential oil of ginger

Add some colour to a spice-based pot pourri, as well as aroma, with flowers or herbs, such as tansy (right) and rosemary (left).

Beauty Treatments

Traditionally in the West, herbs have had a place in beauty treatments, while spices have been overlooked or considered too hot or pungent. However, some spices do have beneficial cosmetic uses and in the Orient, spices have been associated with beauty, perfume and colour for thousands of years. Bear in mind that certain skin types are more sensitive than others, so test each of the following potions and recipes on a small patch of your skin before you use them.

CLEANSING LOTIONS

These preparations make effective lotions for use on your skin.

Nutmeg For a soothing and firming lotion for breasts, infuse 15g (½oz) of nutmeg in 1l (1¾ pint) of boiling water, then strain. Soak cloths in the liquid and leave on the breasts until the cloths cool. Repeat by warming the liquid.

Horseradish This spice makes a good cleansing lotion to get rid of pimples and blackheads. Slice the root and add to milk – 250g (9oz) of root to 250ml (9fl oz) milk – simmer over a low heat for one hour, then strain. Use the lotion on the face and forehead. Keep this bottled and in the fridge.

Coriander This spice can be used to make a pleasant aftershave. Use 60g (2oz) of coriander seeds with 1 tsp of honey and 500ml (18fl oz) of hot water. Simmer for 20 minutes and cool. Add 1 tbsp of witch hazel and strain into a bottle. Keep the aftershave in the fridge, and it will be especially refreshing.

Fennel Eye Lotion Simmer 50g (2oz) of crushed fennel seeds in 500ml (18fl oz) of water for 30 minutes. Strain and let cool. Use this in an eye bath to relieve inflammation.

Hand Cream

You will need:
- 60g (2oz) vanilla beans
- 250g (9oz) pure lard
- 120g (4oz) gum benzoin
- 120g (4oz) spermaceti (from a pharmacist)
- 500ml (18fl oz) almond oil

Put the vanilla beans and lard in a bowl with the gum benzoin, spermaceti and almond oil. Heat in a *bain marie* – a pan or heat-resistant bowl set over another pan of simmering water – to melt and combine, then cool and use as a moisturising hand lotion. You can also use this as an all-over body lotion for massages.

HAIR PREPARATIONS

Add spices to oils and use them to help to keep your hair clean and healthy.

Clove This makes an excellent preparation with a pleasant scent for hair. Heat 500g (1lb) of benzoate lard with 250ml (9fl oz) of almond oil and 2 tbsp of palm oil. Strain and add, while still warm, 2 tbsp of eau de cologne and 1 tsp of oil of cloves.

Star Anise This is another good preparation for hair. Crush and boil 120g (4oz) of seeds in a cup of water and add the resulting oil to olive oil – use 1 tsp of oil of star anise to 150ml (5fl oz) of olive oil. This helps the growth of new hair.

Saffron For tinting fair hair a rich golden colour, soak one dash of saffron in 500ml (18fl oz) of boiling water. Let cool. The saffron water can be used as a wash after shampooing. Do not rinse – leave the hair wet and allow it to dry naturally.

BEAUTY SOAPS

Soap was first made and used in Rome nearly 3,000 years ago, and you can make your own spicy soaps quite simply.

Basic Soap

You will need:
- 250g (9oz) tallow
- 150ml (5fl oz) soft water
- 2 tbsp caustic soda
- dash of turmeric
- 1 tsp ground caraway
- 1 tsp ground sandalwood powder
- 1 ground clove
- 3 tsp ground nutmeg
- 1 tbsp honey
- 1 tbsp olive oil

Melt the tallow in a pan. Pour the water into a separate pan and add the caustic soda. The caustic and water will react, causing heat, and you will have to allow it to cool down. Let the tallow also cool down. When both are lukewarm, pour the melted tallow and oil into the caustic soda and stir all the while – ideally use a whisk.

Add the dry ingredients (finely ground) and the honey and keep stirring. As you whisk you will suddenly find that your liquid turns into a thick, creamy paste.

This is your soap. Pour it into moulds and let it set for 24 hours. Turn it out from the moulds – by this time it will be quite hard – and leave it in a warm, well-ventilated cupboard for about two weeks to cure. Then your spicy soap will be ready to use. It lathers easily and leaves your skin enriched and smelling aromatic and spicy.

This is a basic soap recipe – you can try experimenting and adding your own choice of spices. The turmeric adds yellow colour, but you might like to try paprika for a red tint or a little finely chopped parsley for green.

Caution

Caustic soda in its dry form will burn if it is allowed to come into contact with skin – wash it off with cold water immediately.

Making your own soap is easy, and makes lovely handmade gifts.

Spices for Health

In the thirteenth century many priests and monks began to devote their time to the search for cures based on natural plants, often grown in their monastery gardens. As Spanish and Portuguese explorers came back from the New World with new plants and spices, these were seized on as miracle cures – in many cases being ascribed powers far beyond their actual healing properties.

However, spices do have a natural warming effect and are of some use against colds, coughs and flu symptoms, as tonics, sedatives, laxatives and for relief from the symptoms of rheumatism.

The following medicinal recipes should be taken only for the very mildest of conditions. Any illnesses that you would not normally treat at home without medical advice should not be treated with spice remedies. Always consult a qualified medical doctor if you are not completely sure or if you do not notice any improvement in your symptoms or condition.

SEDATIVES AND RELAXANTS

If you are having trouble sleeping or feel the need for something to relax you during a period of stress or anxiety, spice teas are a natural, non-addictive and soothing way to help.

Fennel, Dill and Anise Tea To make a relaxing drink before bed that can help you get to sleep, take crushed seeds of fennel, anise and dill – use 1 tsp of each – in 250ml (9fl oz) of hot water. Allow it to steep, then strain and drink.

COLDS AND COUGHS

Spices are warming – and what could be better to ward off the effects of cold winter conditions?

Cayenne Pepper Tea Stir ½ tsp of cayenne pepper into 150ml (5fl oz) of boiling water. Let cool and sip slowly. This is said to ward off a cold before it has had a chance to take hold, and it will certainly warm your whole system. You can substitute hot milk for the water in the tea if you prefer.

Ginger and Honey Tea Stir ½ tsp of dried ginger powder into hot milk and add 1 tsp of honey. This is a warming drink to reduce the symptoms of a cold.

Cardamom Tea To reduce the effects of a winter flu fever, mix 1 tsp of basil with the seeds of one large cardamom pod and ½ tsp of ground cinnamon in 500ml (18fl oz) of boiling water with 1 tsp of sugar. Infuse for 10 minutes and take 125ml (4fl oz) every two hours to reduce fevers and chills and to soothe painful joints.

Anise Tea For soothing a cough and to loosen phlegm infuse 2 tsp of crushed aniseed in 300ml (10fl oz) of boiling water. Drink when cool.

TONICS

Eating any of the sweet peppers increases vitamin C intake to give your body a health boost. You can make teas from other spices to provide a tonic to help strengthen the whole system.

Caraway Tea Take 1 tsp of caraway seeds in 250ml (9fl oz) of hot water.

Caper Tea Take 1 tsp of dried and ground capers in 250ml (9fl oz) of hot water.

Ginseng Tea Add 1 tsp of powdered ginseng to 500ml (18fl oz) of boiling water. Simmer for 15 minutes and sip slowly when cool.

Celery Tea Take 1 tsp of ground celery seeds in 250ml (9fl oz) of hot water.

Fenugreek Tea Take 1 tsp of ground fenugreek seeds in 250ml (9fl oz) of hot water.

NERVOUS TONICS

Aniseed Use aniseed to make a refreshing nerve tonic. If a few drops of aniseed oil are added to your bath water it makes a good remedy for nervous headaches and tiredness. It is also good as a massage oil; add two drops of aniseed oil to two drops of nutmeg and rose and add this all to 1 tbsp of almond oil.

Any warm drink has a soothing effect; fennel seed tea can help you to relax.

DIGESTIVE TONICS

In years gone by, after the winter – a period when all people had to eat were salty, stodgy foods – a good digestive tonic was often needed to cleanse the system and restore a sluggish stomach.

Fenugreek Tea (page 149) Make a tea as a general tonic, and you will find it will also increase appetite.

Digestive Teas You can infuse the seeds of anise, cumin, coriander and caraway to make teas to settle upset stomachs. Any of these seeds can be infused in milk or can be chewed after meals. They also sweeten the breath.

Spicy Brandy Tonic Steep 1 tsp each of crushed fennel, aniseed and caraway seeds in 600ml (1 pint) of brandy with 50g (2oz) sugar. Let the mixture mature for four weeks, shaking occasionally. Strain and bottle. Take 125ml (4fl oz) before meals.

Bitter Brandy Tonic Take this as an aperitif before meals to settle the stomach; if taken half an hour before eating, it stimulates the appetite.

To 1l (1¾ pint) of brandy add 2 tbsp of dried orange peel, 2 tsp of crushed cardamom seeds, ½ tsp of ground cinnamon, ¼ tsp of ground cloves. Bottle this and store it for up to a month. Take 2 tbsp before meals.

Nutmeg Wine Take this as an aperitif half an hour before meals. Add one whole grated nutmeg to 500ml (18fl oz) of red wine. Allow to steep overnight then strain and bottle. Take 2 tbsp before meals.

Ginger and Honey Mulled Wine This is a good digestive tonic for those who suffer from winter chills or have poor appetites. Heat a little red wine, making sure the wine doesn't boil. Add some finely grated ginger according to taste and then leave to cool. Add honey – 1 tsp to each glass. If you want to be able to give this drink to children, boil the wine vigorously for a few minutes to get rid of the alcoholic content.

Cinnamon Milk This will act as a good digestive remedy. Take ½ tsp of ground cinnamon in 250ml (9fl oz) of hot milk with a little honey added. This is good at night because it not only settles the stomach and cures indigestion, but it also induces sleep.

Honey makes treatments more palatable and goes well with soothing and warming drinks.

Cardamom Tea Crush the seeds from one pod of cardamom and add to 250ml (9fl oz) of boiling water. Allow to cool and sip slowly. This relieves indigestion.

Cardamom Coffee In Arab countries this is called *gahwa* and is drunk hot and strong. It is considered so beneficial for settling digestion that you are not allowed to speak while the coffee-drinking ceremony is being carried out because it would only undo all the good work the coffee is doing. Crush green coffee beans and add crushed cardamom pods and seeds with a little ground clove (only a dash) to hot water and boil for two minutes. Strain and serve hot and black with sugar.

Juniper Berry Wine Soak 1 tbsp of juniper berries in 1l (1¾ pint) of white wine. Sweeten with 1 tbsp of brown sugar. Let mature for one week and then strain and drink a glass or two as required.

Syrup of Juniper Berries Take this after meals to settle the stomach. Simmer 100g (4oz) of juniper berries, fresh or dried, and the peel of one lemon in 1l (1¾ pint) of water until they soften. Strain, add 2 tbsp of honey, bring to a boil and simmer until the syrup thickens. You can bottle and use immediately. To keep it fresh, store in the fridge. Take 1 tbsp after meals.

Juniper berries can be used to help digestion and rheumatism.

RHEUMATISM REMEDIES
Cinnamon To relieve the pain of rheumatic joints, add a few drops of oil of cinnamon to olive oil and massage into the affected area to bring relief. Do not massage inflamed or swollen joints.

Juniper Berries These can be used in a tea and taken internally to relieve the pain of rheumatic joints. You can also gently heat juniper berries in olive oil for an hour and allow to cool before use as a pain-relieving massage oil. As above, inflamed or swollen joints should not be massaged.

TOOTHACHE REMEDY
Clove To relieve toothache pain, simply clamp a whole clove to the painful tooth and leave for a while to relieve the pain – and then go straight to a dentist.

Cloves are an ancient and effective remedy for toothache.

Licorice root can help to ease constipation.

LAXATIVES

Either through poor eating habits or stress, we may sometimes experience constipation and the use of laxatives may be necessary. Any long-term need for them should be referred to a qualified medical doctor.

Aniseed and Licorice Laxative
Soak 25g (1oz) of licorice root overnight with six dried figs or prunes – or both if you prefer. In the morning simmer with ½ tsp of aniseed and 1 tsp of honey for 15 minutes. Remove the licorice and eat the fruit for breakfast.

BINDING AGENTS

Again, any long-term need for binding agents to ease or cure diarrhoea should be checked with a doctor.

Allspice Binding Agent Add ½ tsp of crushed allspice berries to 1l (1¾ pint) of water and 1 tbsp of bilberries (soaked overnight). Bring to a boil and simmer gently for a few minutes. Allow to cool and add 1 tsp of lemon juice. Stir. Take a cup every few hours until the symptoms pass.

SPICES FOR ALL-ROUND HEALTH

Star Anise This is a diuretic and appetite stimulant and is also useful for relieving flatulence and nausea.

Licorice This reduces inflammation and spasms, expels phlegm and soothes the bronchial tubes.

Elecampane The warming qualities of elecampane make it a good expectorant and a treatment for bronchitis, asthma and other pulmonary infections.

Dill This is rich in sulphur, potassium and sodium.

Celery A poultice of the leaves of celery can be used externally for fungal infections, and the seeds taken in small quantities internally are good for relieving gout, arthritis and inflammation of the urinary tract.

Horseradish This is a diuretic. It increases perspiration, which can be good for some fevers. It can be made into a poultice to be used externally for wound infections, arthritis and pleurisy.

Dill is rich in essential minerals.

Java Galangal This is a warming digestive and is useful as a remedy for diarrhoea, gastric upsets that are sensitive to cold, and incontinence.

Galangal This can be taken internally for chronic gastritis, digestive upsets, gastric ulcerations and to relieve the pain of rheumatism.

Galangal can soothe gastric discomfort.

Mustard This can be used in the form of mustard plasters – bandages soaked in mustard, and applied as a poultice to relieve rheumatism, muscular pain and chilblains. They can be used to soak feet for relief from aches and strains and also to cure headaches and colds; use cold water to maximise the heating effect. People with sensitive skin should take care with this treatment, because it can cause blistering. In large doses it causes vomiting.

Safflower This can be taken as a tea and is good for coronary-artery disease and menopausal and menstruation problems.

Capers These are used to revitalise and increase digestion and stimulate the appetite. They are good for gastrointestinal infections and diarrhoea.

Chillies These are revitalising, help digestion and have a strong stimulant effect.

Cayenne You can infuse cayenne to make a hot, fiery tea to stimulate the appetite and to relieve stomach and bowel pains and cramps.

Sweet Peppers These contain large amounts of vitamin C. They also have revitalising and antiseptic qualities and stimulate the digestive system.

Paprika The warming qualities of paprika make it effective as a reliever of cold symptoms as well as a rich and valuable source of vitamin C.

Caraway These seeds can be chewed for immediate relief of indigestion and colic as well as menstrual pains and cramps.

Grains of Paradise The seeds are used internally in western Africa for a wide range of ailments including painful menstruation and excessive lactation.

Cassia This is a major ingredient in cold remedies and is used for treating dyspepsia, flatulence and colic.

Coriander The leaves are a useful remedy for minor digestive problems, and the coriander seeds can reduce the effects of some laxatives, which can produce painful stomach spasms.

Coriander leaves can help with an upset digestion.

Cumin Minor digestive disorders may be helped if cumin is taken internally. It settles stomach upsets that cause migraines.

Turmeric Taken internally, turmeric is good for digestive upsets and skin disorders.

Lemongrass This can be taken internally by small children as a digestive aid. It can also be taken for mild fevers.

Cardamom Taken internally, cardamom settles upset stomachs and counteracts the effects of dairy product allergies.

Cloves Because they are a warming stimulant, cloves are useful for stimulating the digestive system. They can be taken internally for gastroenteritis and nausea, gastric upsets that are sensitive to cold, and impotence.

Asafetida This cleans and restores the digestive tract and relieves stomach pains and colic.

Fennel This relieves digestive disorders and reduces inflammation. It can be taken as a mouthwash and gargle for sore throats and ulcerated gums.

Juniper This can be used for urinary tract infections – cystitis, urethritis and inflammation of the kidneys – as well as for gout and rheumatism.

Mace This can be used to treat stomach disorders such as diarrhoea, dysentery and indigestion.

Lemongrass can cool a fever and help to soothe children with upset stomachs.

Nutmeg is excellent for the digestion.

Nutmeg In small doses, nutmeg is a carminative, meaning it reduces flatulence and digestive discomfort. It is useful in treating flatulence and vomiting and for improving overall digestion.

Myrtle This reduces colic, flatulence and digestive discomfort, is an expectorant and is helpful in all types of chest infections.

Nigella These seeds are said to benefit digestion and reduce inflammation or irritation in the gut lining.

Opium Poppy This is useful for treating cystitis and pyelitis.

Quassia This is used to treat rheumatism and fevers as well as stomach disorders and dyspepsia.

Allspice The oil of allspice is distilled and used for flatulent indigestion. It improves overall digestion and has a tonic effect on the nervous system.

Aniseed The warming and stimulating properties of aniseed make it useful for treating circulation problems and digestive disorders.

Fenugreek These seeds can be infused to treat gastric

inflammation, colic, insufficient lactation, poor appetite and digestive disorders.

Cubeb Because of its warming properties, cubeb will relieve coughs and bronchitis, sinusitis and throat infections.

Pepper This is very good for stimulating the digestion, warming the bronchial passageways and relieving the congestion of colds and flu.

Sumac This is sometimes prescribed herbally for treating severe diarrhoea, and the root bark is used to treat dysentery. The fruits are used for treating urinary infections.

Sesame These seeds are used as a mild and gentle laxative.

White Mustard This is used to treat bronchial congestion, colds, coughs and rheumatic joint pains.

Tamarind This makes an excellent laxative – its action is fairly gentle. It is also used to treat fevers, asthma, jaundice and dysentery.

Vanilla This has few medicinal uses apart from aiding digestion and improving appetite.

Ginger Recent research has shown ginger to be excellent for settling the stomach, and it is now used as a travel sickness remedy.

Curry The bark of the curry plant is used internally for digestive problems and the leaves are used as an infusion for constipation and colic.

Szechuan Pepper This is a stimulant that works on the spleen and stomach. It also has properties that can lower blood pressure.

Saffron You can infuse saffron to make an herbal tea that can be taken as a warming soothing drink to clear the head. It can also shake off drowsiness and bring on menstruation.

Cinnamon This strong stimulant of the glandular system helps relieve stomach upsets. It is very warming, so it is good for relieving the symptoms of colds, flu and sore throats.

A tea made with saffron is an effective pick-me-up.

Glossary

Addison's disease Disease caused by the underactivity of the adrenal glands

Adrenal glands Glands situated just above the kidneys

Adrenaline Hormone secreted by the adrenal gland that is released in response to physical and mental stress and initiates a variety of responses, including increasing the heart rate

Analgesic Relieves pain

Anaemia Deficiency of haemoglobin in the blood

Antiallergy Reduces allergic reactions

Antibacterial Prevents the formation of bacteria

Antibiotic Prevents the growth of bacteria

Anti-depressant Alleviates depression

Anti-inflammatory Reduces inflammation

Antimicrobial Destroys pathogenic microorganisms

Antiseptic Prevents the growth of bacteria

Antispasmodic Relieves muscle spasms or cramps

Aphrodisiac Increases sexual desire

Aromatherapy Therapeutic use of essential oils usually through massage

Bacteriostatic Prevents the growth of bacteria

Bitters Herbs that have a bitter taste that stimulate the appetite and aid digestion

Carminative Relieves flatulence and settles the digestive system

Cholagogic Stimulates the flow of bile into the intestine

Cicatrisant Promotes the healing of skin and formation of scar tissue

Colic Abdominal pain in the intestines

Cortisone-like action Reduces inflammation

Cystitis Painful inflammation of the bladder

Decongestant Helps eliminate nasal congestion

Diaphoretic Promotes sweating

Diuretic Stimulates the secretion of urine

Douche Application of liquid into the vagina

Dyspepsia Indigestion

Elixir Tincture with added sugar or syrup

Emmenagogue Stimulates menstruation

Essential oils Base materials in aromatherapy that are highly aromatic and volatile and are produced from plants by means of extraction, usually distillation

Expectorant Helps to expel mucus and relieves congestion in the digestive tract

Flatulence Large amounts of gas in the stomach and intestines

Flavonoid Substance responsible for the colours yellow and orange in herbs, fruit and vegetables

Histamine Substance released in response to allergic reactions

Holistic Approach that considers the patient's body, mind and spirit

Lactation Secretion of breast milk

Laxative Promotes the evacuation of the bowels

Mastitis Acute inflammation of the breasts

Mucilage Viscous liquid that forms a protective layer over the mucous membranes and skin

Nervine A nerve tonic that calms the nerves

Neuralgia Acute nerve pain

Osteoporosis Loss of bone tissue

Phlegm Mucus secreted by the respiratory tract

Pleurisy Inflammation of the pleural membrane that surrounds the lungs

Rhizome Underground rootlike structure used as a food store by plants during the winter

Saponin Substance that forms a lather when mixed with water that is found in a variety of herbs and has a wide range of therapeutic properties

Sedative Relieves nervousness and induces sleep with a calming effect

Serotonin Hormone released from the pituitary gland in the brain

Sinusitis Inflammation of the sinuses

Tonic Herbs to strengthen and invigorate a specific organ, system or the whole body

Volatile Evaporates very easily when exposed to air

Index

A

acne 78
aftershave 46, 146
alcoholism 84
alino criolo 129
allspice 86–7, 154
  Binding Agent 152
American mustard 98, 138
Anaheim chilli 134
ancho chilli 135
Andalusian Gazpacho 31
anaemia 69
anaesthetics 86, 106
angina 43
anise 88–9, 148, 150
  Fennel, Dill and Anise Tea 148
anise pepper *see* Szechuan pepper
aniseed 88–9, 149, 154
  Cakes 89
  and Licorice Laxative 152
  oil of 66
antibacterials 33, 106
antiseptics 31, 86, 90, 153
antispasmodic 61
aphrodisiac 14
appetite 21, 28, 34, 43, 46, 50,
  66, 69, 84, 100, 103, 104, 108,
  150, 152, 153, 155
arak 88
arthritis 22, 25, 152
asafetida 60–1, 154
asthma 69, 90, 100, 152, 155
athlete's foot 54

B

Banana Custard with Nutmeg,
  Baked 77
Basque Piperade 131
beauty treatments 146–7
bell fruit *see* sweet peppers
Bhaji, Spinach and Galangal 19
binding agents 152
bird's eye chilli 134
bird's foot *see* fenugreek
bitters 84
blackheads 146
bladder problems 66
  see also cystitis
blood pressure 22, 64, 106, 155
boils 97

Bordeaux mustard 138
Bouquet Garni 116
bowel pains and cramps 34, 153
Brandy Tonics 150
breastfeeding *see* lactation
breasts, firming 146
breath sweeteners 21, 66, 69, 150
bronchial passageways 62, 64, 92,
  98, 155
bronchitis 61, 69, 90, 152, 155
bruising 38, 78
butters, spice 112

C

caffeine 56
Cajun mix 36, 129
Californian chilli 134
capers 28–9, 149, 153
  Caper Sauce 29
capsaicin 34
caraway 40–1, 113, 149, 150, 153
cardamom 56–7, 148, 151, 154
  Coffee 151
  Honey Dressing 126
  Ice Cream 125
carminatives 76, 78, 154
cassia 42–3, 153
catarrh 16
cayenne 33, 34–5, 112, 135, 148,
  153
celery 22–3, 149, 152
chest infections 78, 154
chicken
  Mole Poblano 136
  Tikka Masala 123
chilblains 27, 34, 153
chillies 8, 32–5, 112, 113, 130,
  132–7, 153
  cayenne 135
  Chili con Carne 35
  chilli powder 33
  chilli vinegars 141
  dried 135, 137
China root *see* galangal
Chinese five-spice 43, 128–9
Chinese pepper *see* Szechuan
  pepper
Chinese Salad Dressing 115
Chinese sumac 95
chipotle 134

cholesterol 38, 64
Chutney, Sweet Pepper 118–20
Cider Dressing 115
cider vinegar 140
cinnamon 44–5, 151, 155
  cassia *see* cassia
  Chinese *see* cassia
  Cinnamon Milk 150
circulatory system 52, 88, 154
  blood pressure 22, 64, 106,
  155
  cholesterol 38, 64
citral 54
cleansing lotions 146
cloves 58–9, 146, 151, 154
codeine 82
coffee 56
  Cardamom 56, 151
  Iced Vanilla 105
colds and chills 27, 33, 37, 43,
  44, 54, 98, 106, 148, 153, 155
colic 20, 21, 40, 43, 61, 66, 73,
  103, 108, 153, 154, 155
Colorado chilli powder 134
Compote, Winter 126
congestion 61, 62, 64, 92, 98,
  155
Conserve, Juniper 71
constipation 61, 66, 73, 152,
  155
contraceptives 103
convalescence 97
coriander 46–7, 112, 113, 146,
  150, 153
  Roman *see* nigella
  vinegar 141
coronary artery disease 38, 153
cosmetics 76, 81, 86, 97, 102
coughs 28, 90, 95, 98, 148, 155
cramps 34, 40, 153
cubeb 90–1, 155
cumin 33, 50–1, 150, 154
  black *see* nigella
  Butter 112
  kala 50
  safed 50
  Spicy Drink with 51
curries 121–4
Curry Paste 122
curry powder 128

curry leaf 72–3, 155
curry plant 73, 155
cystitis 82, 154

D
dairy products, allergy to 57, 154
dandruff 84
date of India see tamarind
desserts 125–6
devil's dung see asafetida
diarrhoea 16, 28, 43, 75, 95, 152, 153, 154, 155
digestion 18, 43, 46, 50, 52, 54, 61, 62, 70, 73, 76, 86, 88, 100, 103, 104, 153, 154–5
digestives 21, 22, 28, 31, 33, 43, 59, 69, 81, 92, 150–1, 154, 155
Dijon mustard 138
dill 20–1, 113, 152
    Fennel, Dill and Anise Tea 148
diuretics 25, 66, 106, 152
dizziness 97
drowsiness 49, 155
dry skin 97
Dusseldorf mustard 139
dysentery 61, 75, 95, 97, 100, 154, 155
dyspepsia 43, 84, 153, 154

E
elecampane 68–9, 152
English mustard 98, 138
English whole-grain mustard 139
evil eye 88
expectorants 61, 64, 69, 78, 88, 152, 154
eye lotion 146

F
flatulence 18, 40, 43, 61, 66, 76, 86, 108, 152, 153, 154
fagara see Szechaun pepper
fennel 62–3, 113, 154
    eye lotion 146
    Fennel, Dill and Anise Tea 148
    Florence 62
    Roman (vulgar) 62
fenugreek 102–3, 150, 154–5
fertility 14

fevers 25, 38, 54, 84, 98, 100, 148, 152, 154, 155
five-spice, Chinese 43, 128–9
Florence fennel 62
Florida mustard 139
flower pepper see Szechuan pepper
flu 44, 106, 148, 155
four-spice 127, 129
French mustard 138
fungal infections 54, 152

G
gahwa 151
galangal, lesser 18–19, 153
    Java 16–17, 153
    and Spinach Bhaji 19
galingale see Java galangal
garam masala 50, 127, 128
gargles 62, 69, 95, 154
garlic 8, 33, 113
gastrointestinal system 16, 46, 59, 106, 153, 154–5
    gastritis 18, 153
    gastroenteritis 59, 154
    infections 28, 153
    inflammation or irritation 81, 103
    sluggish stomach 84, 150
    stomach cramps and spasms 46, 153
    stomach disorders 44, 50, 57, 75, 84, 90, 108, 150, 154, 155
    stomach pains 34, 61, 153, 154
    ulcers 18, 64, 153
Gazpacho, Andalusian 31
German mustard 138
gin 70
ginger 108–9, 155
    and Honey Mulled Wine 150
    and Honey Tea 148
    Siamese see Java galangal
    vinegar 141
Ginseng Tea 149
glandular system 44, 155
gonorrhoea 90
goulash 36
gout 22, 25, 70, 152, 154
grains of paradise 14–15, 153
Greek clover see fenugreek
gripe water 20–1

Guacamole 136
guajillo chilli 135
gui zhi see cassia
Guinea grains see grains of paradise
gums 18
    see also mouth ulcers

H
habanero chilli 134
hair preparations 97, 146
halva 102
hand cream 146
hay fever 90
headaches 27, 76, 97, 149, 153
    migraines 50, 154
heartburn 64
haemorrhoids 46, 78, 95
Herb Mustard 99
herpes 69
horseheal see elecampane
horseradish 24–5, 146, 152
    Butter 112
Hottentot tea 73
hu see coriander
hysteria 39

I
Ice Cream, Cardamom 125
Iced Vanilla Coffee 105
impotence 59, 103, 154
incense 66, 144
incontinence 16, 76, 153
Indian chillies 33
Indian mustard 26
indigestion 18, 40, 64, 75, 86, 88, 90, 150, 151, 153, 154
infertility 14
inflammation 62, 64, 152, 154
    of digestive system 70
insect repellent 58
insecticide 54
insomnia 20, 76, 148, 150
intestinal spasms 40

J
jalapeno chilli 134
Jamaican pepper see allspice
Japanese pepper see Szechuan pepper
Japanese quassia 84
Japanese star anise 66, 67
Jarlsberg Bake 15

jaundice 38, 52, 100, 155
Java galangal 16–17, 153
Java pepper see cubeb
joints
   painful or swollen 38, 46, 148
   see also rheumatism
juniper 70–1, 113, 151, 154
   Butter 112
   Conserve 71
   Syrup 151
   Wine 151

K

kala cumin 50
kalonji see nigella
khaa see Java galangal
khas khas 82
kidney disorders 57, 103, 154

L

lactation 14, 21, 62, 81, 103, 153, 155
lal mirch see cayenne
laos see Java galangal
laxatives 38, 46, 62, 64, 97, 100, 152, 153, 155
Lemon and Lime Relish 120
lemongrass 54–5, 113, 154
lesser galangal 18–19, 153
liang-tiang see Java galangal
lice 54
licorice 64–5, 152
   and Aniseed Laxative 152
liver disorders 52
love-in-a-mist 81
lumbago 34, 66

M

mace 74–5, 76, 154
malaguetta chilli 134
malt vinegar 140
marjoram 33
massage oils 146, 149
Mayonnaise, Mustard 139
measles 38
menopause 38, 153
menstruation 14, 38, 40, 52, 102, 153
   stimulating 49, 69, 155
methi 102
migraines 50, 154
Milk Posset 114

Mole Poblano 136
morning sickness 100, 108
morphine 82
motion sickness 108, 155
moutarde de meaux 139
mouth ulcers 18, 95, 154
mouthwashes 62, 69, 154
mulato chilli 135
Mulled Wine 114
   Ginger and Honey 150
muscular pain 27, 153
mustard 112, 138–9, 153
   American 98, 138
   black 26–7, 98
   Bordeaux 138
   brown 26–7, 138
   coarse grain 139
   Dijon 138
   English 98, 138
   English whole-grain 139
   Florida 139
   French 138
   German 138
   green peppercorn 139
   Herb Mustard 99
   Indian 26
   moutarde de meaux 139
   Mustard Butter 112
   Mustard Mayonnaise 139
   mustard vinegar 141
   tarragon 139
   white 98–9, 138, 155
   white wine 139
myrtle 78–9, 154

N, O

nausea 59, 66, 100, 152, 154
nervous system 86, 98, 149, 154
neuralgia 34
New Mexican chilli 134, 135
nigella 80–1, 154
   Noodles with Poppy seeds 83
North American sumac 95
nutmeg 74, 76–7, 146, 154
   Baked Banana Custard 77
   Wine 150
oedema 103
oils, spice 112–13
oily skin 54
opium poppy 82–3, 112, 154
osteoporosis 97
ouzo 88

P

palpitations 43
paprika 8, 30, 36–7, 153
   Butter 112
pasilla chilli 135
pastis 66, 88
pepper 92–3, 113, 155
   anise see Szechuan pepper
   black 92–3
   cayenne see cayenne
   flower see Szechuan pepper
   green 92–3, 139
   Jamaican see allspice
   Japanese see Szechuan pepper
   Java see cubeb
   melegueta see grains of paradise
   pink 92
   sweet see sweet peppers
   Szechuan 106–7, 155
   tailed see cubeb
   white 92–3
perfume 145
perspiration, inducing 25, 38, 39, 152
pharyngitis 90
piccalilli 52
pickling vinegars 116, 140
pimentos see allspice; sweet peppers
Piperade 131
pisihui see cayenne
pleurisy 25, 152
poblano chilli 134
podophyllotoxin 70
pomanders 58
Pontefract cakes 64
poppy 82–3, 112, 154
pot pourri 39, 43, 78, 145
psoriasis 78
pulmonary infections 69, 152
pumpkin pie mix 129
pyelitis 82, 154

Q

quassia 84–5, 154
   Japanese 84
   Surinam 84
quatre-épices 127, 129

R

Ratatouille 130
relaxants 144–5, 148
relishes 118–20

respiratory disorders   16, 25, 52, 57
rheumatism   18, 22, 27, 34, 43, 66, 70, 84, 98, 151, 153, 154, 155
rice
    Hot Indonesian   91
    Spicy   124
ringworm   52, 54
Roman coriander *see* nigella
Roman fennel   62
roundworms   84

S

safed cumin   50
safflower   38–9, 153
saffron   48–9, 146, 155
    bastard *see* safflower
salad dressings   115
sambal   129
Satay Sauce   41
scabies   54, 69
scabwort *see* elecampane
sciatica   98
Scotch bonnet chilli   134
sedatives   20, 148
sereh see lemongrass
serrano chilli   134
sesame   96–7, 112, 155
Shrimp, Szechuan-battered   107
Sicilian sumac   94–5
sinusitis   78, 90, 155
skin problems   18, 22, 38, 52, 69, 154
    cleansers   146
    dry skin   97
    fungal infections   22, 54, 152
    oily skin   54
    psoriasis   78
smallage *see* celery
soaps   147
sore throat *see* throat
sores   52, 69
spasms   64, 152
spice combinations   127–9
spicy vinegars   141
Spinach and Galangal Bhaji   19
spleen   106, 155
sprains   38
star anise   66–7, 88, 146, 152
    Japanese   66, 67
stimulants   33, 52, 59, 106, 153, 155

stinking dung *see* asafetida
stomach *see* gastrointestinal system
sumac   155
    Chinese   95
    North American   95
    Sicilian   94–5
suntan oil   97
Surinam quassia   84
sweet peppers   8, 30–1, 112, 113, 130–1, 153
    Chutney   118
    Grilled   131
paprika *see* paprika
Szechuan pepper   106–7, 155
    Battered Shrimp   107

T

Tabasco   33
tailed cubebs *see* cubeb
tailed pepper *see* cubeb
tamarind   100–1, 155
    Tamarind Water   101
tarragon mustard   139
teas
    anise   148, 150
    aniseed   88
    caper   149
    caraway   149, 150
    cardamom   148, 151
    cayenne   148, 153
    celery   149
    coriander   150
    cubeb   90
    cumin   150
    digestive   150
    elecampane   69
    fennel, dill and anise   148
    fenugreek   149, 150
    ginger   108
    ginger and honey   148
    ginseng   149
    Java galangal   17
    juniper   151
    myrtle   78
    quassia   85
    safflower   39
    saffron   49, 155
    Spicy Herb   63
    sumac   95
throat, sore/infected   44, 62, 64, 90, 95, 108, 154, 155
tiredness   149
tonics   84, 149–50

toothache   59, 151
toothpaste   88
travel sickness   108, 155
tumours, uterine   52
turmeric   48, 52–3

U

ulcers
    gastric   18, 64, 153
    mouth   18, 95, 154
urethritis   154
urinary tract
    incontinence   76
    inflammation/infections   22, 25, 90, 95, 152, 154, 155
uterus
    spasms   40
    stimulants   70, 103
    tumours   52

V, W, Z

vanilla   104–5, 155
vermouth   69
vinegars   116, 140–1
vomiting   76, 154
whooping cough   61
wine vinegar   140
Winter Compote   126
Worcestershire Sauce   52, 141
worms   84
wounds   25, 52, 69, 152
zahtar   129